INNER VICTORY

Winning Strategies
for Managing Life's Transitions

David A. Christensen

CAPACITY BOOKS

Copyright 1995 by David A. Christensen

All rights reserved. No part of this book may be reproduced or transmitted in any form or by any means, electronic or mechanical, including photocopying, recording, or by any information storage and retrieval system, without permission from the publisher except for brief excerpts used in media reviews.

ISBN 0-87411-810-7

Printing Number: 7

Printed in the United States of America

For information or additional copies contact:

Capacity Books
P.O. Box 131
Rexburg, ID 83440
www.davidachristensen.com

ACKNOWLEDGMENT

This book is dedicated to the many seminar participants in my corporate training experience, who encouraged me to produce something to benefit others at "crossroads and new beginnings" in their personal and professional quests. To my many students who continue to inspire me with their insights and their willingness to engage in a lifelong pursuit of personal improvement. To my associates and colleagues who have been supportive of my efforts to try new approaches to helping others along their way in their life's transition points. Last but not least, to my very best friends (my wife, six daughters, two sons, sons and daughters-in-law, and grandchildren) who have given me the desire to undertake a constant personal developmental journey of my own.

CONTENTS

Chapter One

INTRODUCTION

Passing from one condition, form, stage, activity, or place to another is Webster's definition for the word "transition." It is interesting to note that Webster's New World Thesaurus gives several synonyms for the word "transition" which include "shift," "passage," "turn," and "change." The most intriguing synonyms, however, are expressed by the words "development," "transformation," and "realignment." This book is for people who are in TRANSITION. It is for those who are passing from one condition, stage, or activity to another. It is written for those who find that "change" is either necessary, important, advisable—or all three. This book is for students who understand that the move from high school to college is one of the most important transitions they'll experience in terms of laying the foundation for successful living. It is for the graduating university students who will soon be on the doorstep to a new career and yet feel that their education may have taught them how to make a living but somehow forgot to teach them how to live. It is for those who are crossing the line from nuptial bliss to the daily task of building a marriage relationship that will last. It is for those who are experiencing transition forced by loss of employment, divorce, or who have come to the realization that now is the time to make some professional, domestic, or spiritual course corrections in their life's journey. It is for both the rich and famous who somehow feel that they have spent their lives in the "thick of thin things" and desire a transition into a simpler, more meaningful life. It is for the wonderful masses of common people who hear an inner whispering which prompts them to know they can be more than they are.

In short, this book is for everyone! All of us are either in quiet transition, the storm of tumultuous change, or simply find within ourselves a prompting that we must seek a different, more peaceful avenue upon which to travel the rest of our lives. However, in all transitional cases, somehow the synonymous words "development," "transformation," and "realignment" need to take their proper, prominent position in the mindset of all who experience change. Transition is wonderful! If embraced as a friend, and coupled with courage to listen and follow intuitive inner arousal, it can be one of the greatest transformational realignment periods of one's existence. Transition will launch our lives toward long-term growth and development.

You have apparently chosen to accept the inner invitation or that of another to read this book. You, as the reader, should know that this author writes from the perspective of experience. I have both experienced many personal transitions and observed them occurring in the lives of others. In many ways I guess you could say that I have made it a lifelong project to study people in transition. Based on my personal experience, observation, and study, I will share with you my findings in the hope that it will assist you in yours.

More than a few decades ago, I experienced what many young men have and will yet experience—when I took my bride of one year to the hospital to give birth to our first child. It was exciting! I will never forget that day in April when after all the Lamaze classes and birthing preparations, my wife gave birth to a baby girl. I am sure the world stood still for just a moment as I took that little baby, within moments of its entry into the world, and gazed into her perfect little face. All other newborns I had ever seen were pink and ugly, but this little princess was pink and very beautiful. I knew I had something to do with that miracle. At that special moment in time, I felt in my heart that illusive phenomenon for which we all search—"Happiness" or "Inner Peace."

We took that little child into our lives and determined that we would do everything in our power to provide her with not only the necessities, but a life complete with all the wonderful things it has to offer—love, learning, a sense of belonging, and encouragement to embrace living with an eye toward growth and opportunity. I will always remember that day when she reached out with that perfect little hand and grabbed my big nose and said "Da Da." This little miracle started to talk and to crawl and creep. She began to respond not only to love and caring, but to instruction, invitation, and opportunity.

We noticed, however, at about age eighteen months, she stopped talking and began to exhibit some mannerisms which brought us deep concern. We naturally did what anyone else would do. We took her to a pediatrician for a check up. He agreed that there was a problem and wisely sent us to a specialist. For the next fourteen years, we went to over thirty different specialists, each with his or her own solution. Meanwhile our daughter was losing ground, falling further and further behind the developmental standards for children her age. Each doctor gave emphatic assurance that he or she had the answer that would cure her problem. One doctor was certain that she had a brain allergy, however the next "specialist" labeled the previous diagnosis and prescriptive resolution as "quackery" and assured us that his perspective was more valid and would then prescribe a solution which generated a new hope that she would be back on track within a reasonable period of time. We drove hundreds of miles each week to engage her in therapy which was sure to cure her problem. We would have flown to China, South Africa, or clear around the world to find remedy for her well being. She is now in her thirties "30's", and we feel happy that we have found a proper diagnosis and understanding of her state of being.

However, those fourteen years of listening to and following each of many doctors were frustrating in ways that only those who have experienced it can understand. It seems that every specialist had "the answer"! In retrospect I have been profoundly affected by this experience. I do appreciate doctors, specialists, and professionals of every kind. I appreciate the attention and intention with which they serve mankind. However, I pay my most heartfelt respects to those who are willing to go outside "their solutions" in search for perspectives and information they have yet to discover. They somehow know that most information is incomplete and awaiting to be discovered. I remember after we had consulted with nearly twenty specialists, I found myself wishing that we could somehow create a council or meeting of all twenty and invite them to put away their prejudices and recipes, in order to come up with a collective diagnosis and prescriptive remedy. They all seemed to have a part of the answer. They all had an important perspective, but each were so intent upon singing their own remedial song that they discounted all of the possibilities that were outside their sure cures and quick fixes.

My friends, I first of all want you to know that the contents of this book come from many "specialist" sources. Many authors, speakers, and thinkers have contributed to this effort. However, it is important to at least consider the notion that truth is eternal. Truth is verified fact or principle. Truth, then, can be found, added upon, and added with other truths which give new dynamic insights and perspectives and can have significant impact upon the way we choose to live our lives. In this book I will refrain from giving prescriptive recipes and focus more upon correct principles, processes, and truth or verifiable information which have been helpful in bringing other people to a happier, more fulfilled state in their lives. If truth is eternal, you will not likely find new or revolutionary ideas for your "transition" within the pages of this book. However, hopefully you will discover or rediscover an idea or concept that will accelerate "realignment," "transformation," and "development" in your life. What you read and consider will serve only as a catalyst in helping you to discover customized solutions found within your own heart and mind. You should know that "quick fixes" and "sure cures" do not exist. You should learn to be very suspicious of anything or anyone who purports to have the complete truth in the absence of a willingness to search for, add to, or even multiply truth by truth. You must know that your own commitment is as important as the truth you will discover and embrace. Know that your transition can be and will be facilitated with an appropriate measure of commitment and effort.

I have spent decades as a student of motivation. I have enjoyed many books, audio programs, seminars, workshops, and video presentations on the subject. From each I have personally extracted wonderful ideas and practical concepts for living my life.

I have enjoyed the writings and perspectives of Dr. Denis Waitley, Brian Tracey, Rabbi Harold Kushner, Dr. Stephen R. Covey, and Hyram W. Smith. I have with interest read the views of Lee Iacocca, Jack Welch, and Malcolm Gladwell. I have been lifted by the insights of religious leaders Gordon B. Hinckley and have been moved by the stories of Mahatma Gandhi, Martin Luther, John Huss, and Mohammed, and C.S. Lewis. While a list like this could go on-and-on my personal line-up includes Prophets Moses, Isaiah, Mosiah, and since I am a Christian, the teachings of Jesus Christ and those who have sought to understand and teach of Him—like C.S. Lewis's classic collection The Problem of Pain, The Screwtape Letters, the Great Divorce, and Mere Christianity.

Now, I don't know about you but in the end I have come to appreciate and utilize a select few of them or find an affinity for the things they teach because they line-up with what I perceive to be true. It is the same with all of us. We search and seek to identify with those and their teachings that seem to us to be 'true'. Somehow 'truth' turns our hearts and heads toward a new view or explanation that increases our understanding, causes us to be more disciplined, or helps us make sense out of what seems to be a confusing world at times. To me, in the end, 'truth' is self-evident (without need of proof or explanation), and often it takes time for it's evidence to mount.

While many authors, speakers, and presenters have contributed their ideas to my life and hence the perspectives which have lead to writing this book, it is my hope that you will begin your own search for the truth which will make your life free and happy. "Truth" and true principles were not invented by George Washington, Abraham Lincoln, Martin Luther King, Gandhi, or the

---

wonderful present day authors and speakers on the subject of success. It is important to remember that "TRUTH" has been around a lot longer than any of the people who have sought it, understood it, and ultimately employed it. Just as the many physicians who diagnosed my daughter's condition didn't have the complete truth, so do all of us, fall short in giving complete and total remedy for each individual life. Each of us must execute periodic and searching self-examination while listening to our own inner whisperings. It is the process of our searching and discovering truth and even error that will bring passion and purpose to our lives. This is therefore the purpose of this book, to stimulate the process of personal discovery at whatever transitional stage you are in.

Why This Book?

Several years ago I was personally forced to face my own life squarely and make a course correction. I loved to teach, to write, to study and develop ideas. I feel that I was a good teacher and was told by those I taught that they had found that their lives were positively influenced by what had happened in my classroom. However, the economics and financial remuneration of teaching coupled with the growing expenses of meeting my aforementioned daughter's medical needs prompted a change or transition. Somewhere in that transition my enjoyment of life and capacity to contribute to the world around me began to veer off. My values did not change nor did I ever compromise deep-seated principles, but in time, my focus began to shift away from who I really was. After some years of prosperity, meeting the medical economic demands of our daughter, and building what appeared to be a great financial success story, the national economy slid significantly backwards and our financial world toppled around us. Even in the prosperous eras of my life, I felt I was falling short of what I call "employment enjoyment." I didn't really enjoy the day to day combat of running a large and growing business. It was during these difficult times that it became evident that we needed to evaluate the course we were pursuing and make yet another correction. Over time, my search resulted in a transition back into teaching, though this time it was in the corporate arena as a corporate trainer. It had never occurred to me that teaching could be both a rewarding and lucrative proposition.

I again enjoyed life and living. I spent my life teaching men and women in their thirties, forties, fifties, and those approaching the sunset years of retirement. The message of our training was about Time, Priorities, Values, and Course Corrections. Day after day, seminar after seminar, workshop after workshop, the teacher (me) was being taught. I began to perceive a common response to the process and instruction we gave. There was no consistent age, gender, nor success factor in my observations. At the conclusion of each seminar, there was always a significant contingent of seminar participants who would linger around after the others had departed the training room. They voiced the similar concerns, observations, and questions which I had encountered in my own transitional discomforts:

> "I am making a nice six-figure income, I have been working for this company for twenty-five years, but I am not happy!"

> "I wish I would have had something like this (training) when I was in college."

> "I enjoy my work for work's sake, I have been treated well by my employer, I don't want to change careers, but can you help me change the way I am seeing and living my life? . . . I can't say I really enjoy the "living" part of life. . . ."

> "How can I get the courage to change what I know needs to be fixed?"

Over and over again the same kind of comments and questions surfaced. Seeing that so many people were indicating concern, I started to wonder about the other members of the class who sat and made no comments at all. Were they in agreement with the comments being given? Were they just shy, reserved, or not so verbal in their behavioral style? So I asked them and began to see an important trend. For most, if not all people, "Transition" or shift, change, and course correction toward realignment, transformation and development are a constant! We are all in need of checking "where we are" with "who we are" and "why we are" and "what we are doing." This new view made me see my own "transitions" differently. In fact, a new idea emerged in my thinking process. In retrospect I could see that I had experienced some major career changes in my life, but the real solution was in learning to live each day with enough understanding of who, what, why, and how I would live. With that perspective, life would merely be a series of 365 micro-transitions per year. In other words, realignment and correcting our course in life is a daily exercise. It is the constant "checking" to insure that "who I am" is in sync with "why I am" and "what I genuinely want life to be."

Then came the clincher. Remember, I am answering the question, "Why this Book?" The summer season came and one of my clients hired several hundred college students for internship experiences. Students in their third or final year of university education were hired by General Motors to work for two to four months to enhance their education with valuable experience while being paid—a very nice thing for both the company and the students. The training director for one particular division of that company in Detroit invited me to teach my workshop to several groups of those in internship assignments. I suppose if there was a time when I decided this book needed to be written, it was in this summer intern encounter with wonderful students at General Motors in Detroit. At the conclusion of each of many one-day workshops with different groups of university students from a variety of institutions like Ohio State, UCLA, Notre Dame, Florida, and a host of smaller liberal arts schools, the comments made by these students (ten, twenty, and thirty years behind my older and wiser corporate students) had a familiar ring.

"I wish I would have had something like this (training) when I was starting college."

"I am six months from graduation in a career I am not sure I really want to pursue or think I will find enjoyment, what should I do?"

"I have learned the discipline of engineering and think I can make a nice living at doing it, but I sense there is more to life than designing next year's new car—what can I do to learn how to live?"

Isn't it interesting that young adults in the twilight of their university experience and at the dawning of their productive lives were sensing that they were starting off course? I decided I would at least make an attempt to create something that could potentially assist young and mature adults alike to consider thinking about life and designing a course to cue into a compass which would help them navigate the micro transitions and realignments of daily living.

How?

Let's identify how this book can really make a difference in your life. Since you are reading this book, it is safe to say that you have either been assigned by someone to do so or someone has recommended it to you, **or** you independently chose to read it after picking it up and thumbing through the pages. 'Whatever your motivation, I know that the information in this book if applied can make a significant difference in your life. Why will this book be different from any one of a thousand others on the same subject? Because you will do more than just sit down and read it. It will serve more as a guidebook to assist you in the designing for yourself a better more focused life, and a compass that will assist you in your daily navigation.

Early in my life, my father left the farm and obtained a contractor's license. Night after night, I would observe him bring home set after set of blueprints. He would remove the rubber band holding a set in a roll, lay them out on the kitchen table, and spend hours reviewing, looking at, checking, and finally making critical computations that became his bid price to construct the building. After a few years I learned from him how to look at the plans and make some sense out of them. I learned that behind the front cover sheet there was generally an elevation page where I could catch a glimpse of what the building would look like from the front, back, sides, and top. That was usually followed by a page which identified the floor plan or what the building would look like from the top looking down. Careful review gave important insights like dimensions, room names and uses, and so forth. Next, the several pages which followed identified the specifics or details of the foundation construction, how much concrete, how much steel, grade and thickness of concrete, and exact placement of steel rebar and connective reinforcements. Other pages each exhibited in similar detail, roof structure, electrical, plumbing, insulation, floor covering, window, and fixture. I remember feeling some fascination with how anyone could create such a detailed rendering of something seen only in the mind of the architect doing the drawing.

At the job site on a fairly routine daily or hourly basis, I observed builders, inspectors, and vendors come on the premise and refer over and over again to the blueprints. Never did I witness a subcontractor just start digging a foundation, rough in a plumbing system, or construct a roof without consulting the blueprint. I do remember a time or two when some overanxious worker made a mistake by either not reading the plan correctly or assuming incorrectly from previous experience on another job site with construction specifications from a different set of drawings for a different building. It would have been easy to say, "Oh it's all right, let's just leave it this way" and move on. I am sure you know what happened. The incorrect portion was usually torn down and removed and then redone according to specifications in every detail.

The purpose of this book is to aid you in designing a set of blueprints for your life. We will call this blueprint your Personal Creed Document. It will include, among other things which you choose to add, your mission statement, details regarding your values, specifics of your goals, and other important information to guide you in your life.

It is hard to imagine anyone thinking that a beautiful building could be constructed without a set of blueprints to guide its builders through the construction phase. It is just as inconceivable to contemplate the creation of a beautiful life without design and emphasis to why, what, and how we are doing it. In many ways it is a tragedy that human beings, who have such an incredible potential to enjoy success and happiness, live life without much thought for building something uniquely beautiful. Why do the masses of humanity live as Thoreau once said, "lives of quiet desperation"? Why will most people spend more time planning a birthday party, a Christmas gift list, purchasing an automobile, or writing checks to pay credit card installment debt than designing their life?

The result of not deliberately conceptualizing our lives and considering the things which matter most to create a good one are hundreds of wonderful people like those mentioned earlier in this chapter who shared with me their frustration of coming up short or having strived to achieve things that did not produce the joy and inner peace of living they desired.

You may choose to read this book differently than you have others. Perhaps you will want to read it one chapter per week while you think, ponder, and then act upon the challenges and invitation to create each individual part of your Creed Document. Maybe one quick reading will help you to see the overall picture of where you are going with your Creed Document, followed by a more detailed reading as you design each specific part of the important blueprint for your life. Remember, you are creating a set of blueprints for the way you will live your life.

An important caution should be noted here. The analogy of blueprints being used to create a beautiful building is a graphic and valid way to visualize the intent of this book and the end product which is your Personal Creed Document. However, there are differences between a building and a human. Buildings are stationary and are built for a specific location. People live in a less static circumstance where things, conditions, and situations change. It should be perfectly understood that your Personal Creed Document will change from time to time. This exercise of creating a blueprint for your life is a process. The end result will undergo additional changes and improvements as the years come and go. This is to be expected and appreciated. Another caution in considering the blueprint analogy: Before you ever start a building you must have a plan! You do not need a full set of blueprints complete with detailed drawings and building strategies to start your life. Just start now! Begin today to employ just one of the ideas, concepts, or principles you read about. As your Personal Creed Document grows and becomes more meaningful to you, so will your life. It is all a process and will most likely be one that is never ending.

Commitments

Before we launch into the subject matter, consider a couple of commitments. This experience will be worthless unless you take action and employ the ideas taught. I want to invite you to make two commitments right now.

The first commitment I invite you to make to yourself is:

1. "I will take notes." There is a relationship with what you will get out of this book and your willingness to take notes. I am not going to suggest that you need to take copious or detailed notes unless you demand that of yourself. Just know and understand that research validates the fact that you will get more out of this experience if you are underlining, making marginal notes, or recording ideas which come to your mind as a result of what you read or experience. I believe that as you read, you will be prompted with a thought or idea of how you can personally employ that idea into your life. The idea which comes to you is very important and in my mind may even be of divine origin. WRITE IT DOWN. TAKE NOTES!

2. Share it! Make a commitment to yourself right now that you will teach one idea or concept you learn from each reading or chapter with someone else within the next twenty-four to forty-eight hours. The ideas and concepts you will learn or be exposed to are universal. You can teach them to a roommate if you are in college, to a coworker if you work, or to your loved ones. When we teach someone else what we have learned, we learn twice. There is a validated relationship

between how much you learn and how much you'll employ from what you learn if you share it. Receiving begins the learning process; teaching completes it. Pick one idea from each chapter and determine to whom you will teach it and when you will teach it. It is important that you do this within forty-eight hours of the time you learn about the concept. I will invite you to make other commitments to yourself as we move along. I want to make a commitment to you. I want you to enjoy this experience. I want you to like this book. I want you to say at some future point in your life, "this encounter with myself has made a difference in my life." I want your life to be happier than before we started this journey. I want you to experience at least one "AHA" experience. An AHA experience is one of those quiet stirring moments when your heart and your mind communicate. It is when you read or think something and intuitively sense that it is true or right or good. I commit that I will do my best to convey important insights and thoughts, which when employed can improve your life. I commit to do whatever I can to the end that you enjoy this experience.

Chapter Two
A FOUNDATION FOR THIS EXPERIENCE

The return you receive for your investment of time and energy into reading this book and involving yourself in this experience will be maximized if we pay attention to a few foundational principles at the beginning. These principles will give us a substructure or underpinning upon which we can develop many ideas.

Throughout this book we will be looking at life's critical issues through the windows of three perspectives. Let's identify and define each:

1. **Laws**

    These are universal principles that govern causes and effects in our lives. We cannot and would not want to change or eliminate them. They are natural and provide us a foundation upon which we can operate. It is also important to understand that "laws" don't care! They have no feelings. It does not matter whether we like them or not. For example, there is a physical law on this planet we call gravity. It does not care whether or not we like it. If we jump up, we come down. If we hold a pencil out in front of us and let go, it will fall. Gravity does not care! There are mathematical laws which govern our checkbook. Two dollars minus two dollars will always be zero dollars. Two dollars minus seven will always be a negative five dollars, not twelve, one, or six. My banker may care and lend me money or feel sorry for me if I don't manage my financial resources properly, but laws don't care! There are laws which govern our behavior and create causes and effects in our lives as well. They don't care either, they just are! Likewise we can spend our energy wishing they didn't exist or wishing that they would change so life wouldn't be so much of a challenge. Laws are the universal principles that govern and give predictable structure to the universe.

2. **Arts**

    Arts are the LEARNABLE skills in applying our understanding of the Laws. It is important for us to appreciate and embrace the fact that arts can be learned, developed, and become habitual. We can learn to manage gravity so it assists us in accomplishing. We can become proficient in managing mathematical laws to give us accurate and important information with regards to our bank statements. We can learn to manage the Laws which affect our behavior to the end that we can transform or make positive changes in our lives.

3. **Clues**

    Clues are the evidences of what happens when we either apply or violate the Laws. They are what is left after we have acted. If I drop an expensive ceramic vase from the top of a three-story building onto a concrete sidewalk, I can examine the results to find a conclusive clue which verifies I should not do that unless my objective is to destroy or break the vase into many pieces. If I carefully apply the laws of arithmetic to my checkbook, an examination of the results give evidence that I am never overdrawn on my account and my relationship with my bank and the check payee(s) are enhanced. Successful and happy living leaves a residual trail of clues and likewise so does failure. If we fail to learn from the mistakes which produce failure, we are destined to make the same mistakes and reap their consequential reward. If we seek to find and understand the clues generated by the successful, and employ them rightly in our own lives, we too will experience the harvest of right doing. We will be looking at the clues left by those who have reached admirable levels of success and will challenge ourselves to examine what law or principle governed the cause and effect as well as the action or art which produced it. We will periodically examine the clues left by people whose lives exhibit misery, unhappiness, and failure to see if we can identify which laws were violated, how the person never learned to manage the law, and determine how we might avoid similar outcomes and results in our own lives.

The story is told of one of golf's greatest players. He was playing in a tournament some time ago and was not having a great or productive day in terms of his score. In fact, he was significantly behind the several leaders in the tournament. You see, even a successful golfer who had won more international golf tournaments than anyone else and who was still winning his share on the Senior Circuit had days that were not "successful." In this particular tournament he was extremely frustrated with his performance. He was not hitting the ball with the kind of accuracy and power he was known for. On the ninth or tenth hole, he stepped up and carefully laid the ball on a tee. He stepped back, paused, refocused his mind and attitude, evaluated the environmental issues, and then stepped up and hit the ball perfectly down the fairway to the distant green. The ball bounced, rolled, and stopped just one easy putt from the cup. He knew he had hit a near-perfect shot and the crowd knew it too. You could hear a significant applause from the onlookers in the gallery. This great golfer, while pleased with his shot, was still frustrated in his heart with his overall performance. He picked up his tee and walked toward his caddie who was a few feet from the front line of golf fans viewing the event from the gallery. One well-meaning fan near the caddie congratulated this champion by saying "Wonderful shot! I would give anything to hit a golf ball like you just did." This was not the right day to compliment one of golfs greatest heroes. His frustration gave through and he turned to the spectator and said, "You wouldn't give anything to hit a golf ball like I just did. Do you know what it takes to hit a ball like I just did? I get up every morning at five o'clock, I go out on the golf course and hit a basket of a thousand balls. Do you see this hand?" he invited the fan to look. "This hand starts to bleed. So after I finish hitting the thousand balls, I go to the club house and wash the blood off my hand, slap a bandage on it, and then I go get another basket of a thousand balls and I hit all of them. That's what it takes to hit a ball like I just did! No, you wouldn't give anything to hit a ball like I just did." He later sought out and apologized to the spectator for being so curt and publicly insensitive but this great golfer knew something about "clues," "arts," and "laws." He watched for the clues or evidences of successful golfers, he determined the arts they had applied and hence had developed an understanding of the game. He modeled and mirrored successful golfers over and over until he became one of them.

It is simply unbelievable to observe how the human family has perpetually made the same mistakes and reaped the harvest of doing the same stupid things generation after generation. While each of us make our share of the same mistakes made by our predecessors thus reaping the consequence, I am convinced that we do not need to repeatedly suffer the residue of living out of harmony with the laws that govern us all.

When I was about one year old, I loved to go behind a large coal stove which produced heat for our home. It was situated in one corner of our family room and behind it my parents placed a large coal bucket containing black coal to feed the fire. I loved to negotiate my way to the coal bucket behind the stove and remove each piece from the bucket one by one and scatter it on the floor. My mother was naturally frustrated by the mess I created but more so she was concerned that her toddler might burn himself on the hot furnace.

My mother, father, and five older siblings would instruct: "Don't go behind the stove, you'll get burned!" My mother even took me instructively to the stove and gently assisted me to hold my hand an appropriate distance from the surface of the stove to feel the intense heat radiating from it. She wanted me to understand in some way that it was dangerously hot and should be respected. One day when my mother was in another part of the house and my siblings in school, I repeated a fateful journey to the back of the stove, removed each piece of coal from the bucket, and started my return trip back out into the family room. This time I stumbled, lunging forward in the direction of the stove instinctively holding out my hands to break my fall. The process left me in a leaning position pressing my hands against the surface of the hot furnace. Several precious seconds passed before my mother made it to her screaming toddler and removed my hands from the outer surface of the stove. I am told that much of the scorched flesh stuck to the furnace surface. After emergency room examination and treatment followed by subsequent medical opinions, it was the recommendation of the medical advisors that my hands be removed by amputation. Gratefully that process was not necessary. I live with fully functioning hands marred only by large wax-like scars in the palms and finger tips. May I draw upon this story to illustrate an important point? I may make an effort to justify my error, I may erroneously blame the adults in my life who allowed me to be in the room with a hot stove, or I may excuse myself suggesting that I was not old enough to understand. I can undertake an effort to make lists of reasons why I was burned. There is one overriding fact that really negates all justification. It is a fact that I had at my disposal over one hundred collective years of experience. My parents and my siblings combined had 114 years of understanding the Laws associated with hot stoves. They had learned the art of keeping an appropriate distance from hot surfaces. While none of them had the same kind of encounter with the stove, experience had somehow taught and exhibited evidence or clues of what happens to people who fail to respect fire, hot surfaces, and specifically furnaces. I could have avoided tragedy by paying attention to those clues.

It is important for us to remember that what we are studying in this book comes from the knowledge and understanding of thousands of collective years of experience. The concepts taught are based on true principles. They are not the concepts of David A. Christensen, Hyrum W. Smith, Dr. Stephen

Covey, Dennis Waitley, Anthony Robbins, Wayne Dyer, nor Ralph Waldo Emerson, Thomas Jefferson, Henry David Thoreau, Buddha, or wise King Solomon. These true principles have existed much longer than any of us. They represent thousands, maybe even millions or trillions of years. We can study true and timeless principles and revalidate them by action or inaction. What we individually decide to do about what we learn or come to know is entirely up to us. We have gained sufficient understanding of the Laws by examination of the evidence (clues) and arts (skills) we need to employ to be successful.

The Law of the Harvest

The Law of the Harvest is an important foundational law in life. It is easy to see how the Law of the Harvest is a natural system that really dominates much of what we experience in this life. I recently resided in a state famous for its potatoes. It is fascinating to observe the agricultural community and what it goes through to bring in a crop of potatoes. The most successful farmers spend two, three, or even four years preparing for a single crop. Crop rotation, fertilization and soil treatment are among the many concerns of the farmer. Even more important *is* the careful, watchful eye on unpredictable variables like weather, rain, frost, ground temperature, and so forth. The farmer knows that he or she has a window of two to four weeks to get the seed into the ground, three months to nurture if nature will co-operate, and two to four weeks to get the harvest out of the ground before nature takes over. Nature *is* very unforgiving. It doesn't allow us to "fake it" long term.

What would you say if the all potato farmers on planet earth sent out a sat-ellite advisory via CNN, CBS, NBC, and ABC NEWS to all the *rest* of us saying, "we are sorry, world, but we were busy playing golf or otherwise preoccupied with other things during the planting season and forgot to plant." We might react like this: "You what? You forgot to plant? How could you forget to do something so basic as planting your crop? You stupid farmers!" We also know that it would be ludicrous for us to respond "Well you just better hurry up now and catch up or we won't have anything to eat. . . . speed grow it!" I can see the reaction of my potato-growing friends if we were to say to them, "I know its July and the frost will come in forty-five days but can't you just hurry and plant now and bring in those nice baking potatoes anyway?" To suggest such a remedy is more stupid than their folly of not remembering to plant. You just can't cram on the farm.

Nature doesn't allow for it. In my early years, we lived on a dairy farm. Dairy farmers milk their cows two time each day. It would have been insane to suggest that "instead of milking twice each day, let's just do it once a day—or better yet, let's just milk on Mondays, Wednesdays, and Fridays." Nature and the uncomfortable milk-producing animals would not cooperate. At first their discomfort would be annoying to all concerned and then in time they would simply stop producing milk, and they would "dry up." Natural law takes over and what we harvest would be a direct result of what we did or failed to do. You can't cram on the farm!

Did you ever cram in school? Perhaps you messed around and then in the final hour of the term you crammed a lot of information into your short-term memory ... passed a test ... and then promptly forgot it all. Well, that works as far as getting a grade is concerned, but what about the longterm results? I have noted in my personal experience as a student and more recently as a college professor, "The Law of the Harvest" is Truth. You cannot cram on the farm and if we want a successful semester, season, year, decade, or life in school, marriage, or business, we have got to treat it like the farmer treats his crop. Preparation, planting, and tending to vitally important issues in any endeavor will create a more plentiful harvest. Just as there may be uncontrollable variables that pop in unannounced on the farm, i.e., drought, floods, hail, wind, and etc., life also renders things we cannot control. However the extent to which we prepare, plant properly, and harvest with, intensity will determine our success. Cramming is an incorrect principle. Quick Fixing is an incorrect principle not worthy of any attention. The Law of the Harvest is fundamental to life.

In the long run, the Law of the Harvest governs all arenas of life. We just can't fake it long term. As you consider your "transition," or your invitation to develop, realign, and become a more successful person, maybe it would be a good idea to evaluate where you are in your understanding of the Law of the Harvest or as it is called by some, "The Law of the Farm." Remember Law doesn't care, you do.

The Seeds of "Nothing"

The only caution one might be aware of when thinking about the Law of the Harvest or Law of the Farm, is that where the farmer does not sow, he will not reap or harvest. However, in our lives we are always sowing, even if it is nothing. Do you understand? In our lives "nothing" is both seed and harvest. Sowing seeds of "nothing" may reap a harvest of fiasco.

If I choose to do nothing about my studies in school, a book report due next week, or visit with my lab instructor about a missed assignment, by doing "nothing" I am planting "something" and am sure to reap the harvest of the same. In the harvest, I must expect lower grades, less long term knowledge, and wasted resources.

If I choose to do nothing about preparing for a sales or business meeting that can impact my relationship with a customer or client, I am sowing something called "nothing" and must anticipate the harvest of lost sales, strained business relationship, or maybe even loss of employment.

If I choose to do nothing about spending time enhancing my relationship with my spouse or children, I can anticipate that my harvest of personal capacity to build and influence their lives will be diminished.

The Law of the Harvest is simple, and it is real. Perhaps you should ask yourself two important questions in the transitional concerns of your life.

1. Today I am reaping the harvest of yesterday's planting. What did I plant then and how did I nurture the crop that I am reaping today? In the big transitions of our lives it is easy for us to see what we did wrong or what kind of seeds were sown to produce the crop we reap. Your introspection will enable you to pinpoint "something seeds" or "nothing seeds" that have produced abundantly.

2. If I am happy about today's harvest, am I planting and nurturing my crops in the same manner to the end that I reap the same positive fruit? If I am not pleased with today's crop, what will I do differently to reap something different? An old Chinese proverb defines insanity as "doing the same things in the same way and expecting different results." If I am not happy with the results or outcomes in my life, then I would do well to consider the Law of the Harvest or Farm and identify the seeds or essence of what is creating negative outcomes?

The Law of the Harvest is real. Anyone who would attempt to plant corn seed and expect to harvest peas or sow sunflowers and expect daisies we would declare as derelict or incompetent. Why would we expect anything differently in school, relationships, or business? It is relatively simple to identify the fruits of the harvest and predict next season's yield if we choose to sow the same kinds of seeds. It is simple to understand that we can't plant carrots and produce potatoes. It is equally simple to examine the fruit to determine which seed to sow.

What's Happening in Your Garden?

Art of Personal Inspection

Refine your ability to identify and study seeds and fruits. I am not talking about becoming a seed analyst but I am suggesting that we can all learn the skill of standing back a short distance from the "fruit" (outcome) of daily living, and identifying the "seeds" which were planted to produce the harvest. It takes years to become proficient as a seed geneticist, but anyone can learn to identify the seeds and fruits of human behavior. Masses of humanity never really get past the primary questions of living day to day. Their lives are dominated by questions like:

1. Who do I work for? Do I like my boss?

2. Did I make enough money today to pay my bills? Can I buy a few toys to keep me from being bored?

3. Who do I like and who are my enemies?

4. What should I do next?

5. Will it rain, snow, or shine?

6. When can I go on vacation? When do I have to be back?

7. Is life fair? Why do other people have more than me?

In order to identify seeds and fruit, learn to ask questions about the results you are experiencing in your life. Just as any good analyst will do, first ask general questions and then move to specifics. Maybe you could consider a more effective line of questioning like:

1. Am I happy? Am I satisfied with all of the results in my life today?

2. Do I truly enjoy living? Do I love to get up in the morning?

3. Does my "being" matter to anyone else? Am I leaving a legacy for others?

4. Is there anything missing in my life? Is life full and complete?

5. How is my health? What can I do to improve it?

6. Am I really living life to my potential?

7. Do I feel loved? Do I sense love for others?

8. Am I learning, feeling, sensing, growing?

9. What could I do to increase my enjoyment?

10. Am I really paying attention to vitally important things?

11. Is there something I really feel strongly about? Do I have a passion for something? Is there a crusade I would live and die for?

12. What do I believe?

13. Can I make someone else happy and enjoy life more?

14. Is there anyone I can include in my life that understands my world from the perspective of real life experience?

15. What are my values? What really matters to me?

16. Do I have goals? Are they written down?

17. What can I learn from the experiences of life? Who has taught me important things? What have others taught me by their examples and lives?

18. Do I have hard feelings toward anyone?

19. Does anyone have hard feelings toward me which I have some power to control?

20. What is my song? What will my world remember about me? What am I leaving behind?

As you learn to ask questions about life and living, you are forced to look at seeds and fruits." We ultimately have to think about the seeds we sow, the fruit we harvest, and about our garden. The purpose of subsequent chapters is to help you evaluate and analyze the garden of your life in relation to the various roles you play and to assist you in your transitional concerns. You will be invited to examine your beliefs, think about time, consider who you are and how you relate to others, and be encouraged to understand and embrace the power of mentorship. You will have a chance to evaluate your values in relation to your actions, consider issues relating to goals, and learn about the empowering principles of gratitude and forgiveness.

If you are willing to pay attention, to seek to understand the laws, to invest the time to learn the arts of application and to be aware of the clues of effective living, you will gain a great deal from the experience. Your transition will be more productive and direct you toward a positive developmental new beginning.

Chapter Three

THE STUFF LIFE IS MADE OF

I am convinced that one of the major differences between people who love life and know how to live it to its fullest and those who don't, is couched in the great commodity of TIME. Benjamin Franklin said "to love life is to love time for time is the stuff that life is made of." I feel one of the major differences between those who fail, and those who succeed at nearly anything is the degree of affection which a person has for Time and its implications. I am not talking about "traditional time management" or the ability to get things done. Nor am I talking about an affection for the clock, efficiency, or even planning systems. I am talking about the capacity of successful people to understand and use time as a gift.

Peter Drucker, called by *The Los Angeles Times* "Founding Father of the Science of Management" once stated: "Everything requires time. It *is* the only true universal condition. All work takes place and uses time. Yet most people take for granted this unique, irreplaceable, and necessary resource. NOTHING ELSE, PERHAPS, DISTINGUISHES EFFECTIVE EXECUTIVES AS MUCH AS THEIR TENDER LOVING CARE OF TIME" *(The Effective Executive,* Harper & Row, page 26). Think about the importance of TIME in life. Education, business, medicine, sports, and literally everything is time based.

Even sitting on an ocean pier, looking out to the sea as we find psychic space and are rejuvenated, finds a basis in time. We would do well to inventory and determine how important TIME is in our life. Paraphrasing and combining Drucker's statement with Benjamin Franklin's to fit all of us might look something like this, "nothing else, perhaps, distinguishes effective and happy people more than their affection and tender care of the stuff that life *is* made of."

Let's begin by making an effort to identify what time is. I have always been intrigued with a statement uttered by St. Augustine when he said "For what is time? Who is able, easily and briefly to explain it? Surely we understand well enough when we speak of it. What then is time? If nobody asks me, I know; but if I were desirous to explain it to someone, plainly I know not." Time just exists, doesn't it? When we were young and in school it moved so slowly. It was like an eternity between recesses and even longer until summer vacation or Christmas. Time dragged on! As we get older it seems to fly. We never seem to have enough of it and are constantly forced to make choices relating to it. We work in vain to "save it" and use it as an excuse by saying "we don't have it." We read books and go to workshops to help us manage it. The truth is, we can't save it and we have all there is.

Down through the ages, the phenomenon of Time has been an issue which philosophers have attempted to define. For example, Newton said that time is absolute and the essence of the universe. Leibnitz was not sure what it was but declared what it was not. He taught that it was anything but absolute. Einstein theorized that it was simply a series of events. Webster defined it as a continuum in which events succeed one another from past through present to future." So what is it? Is it twenty-four hours divided into one thousand four hundred and forty, sixty second segments? Or is it simply a man-made handle to which we attach a label so the world can be coordinated? I believe the definition given a few years ago by a young college student who I have come to admire greatly, Greg Williams, comes closer to being a correct definition of time than any other I've ever heard. "Time is a standard or measurement through which we can measure the progression or digression of self or group." Isn't that insightful? Time is not about clocks, minutes, efficiency, or checking things off of a "TO DO" LIST. Time has more to do with progression or digression and is a standard or way of measuring it. Former Utah Supreme Court Justice Dallin Oaks has said, "The issue [of time] is not what we have done but what we have become. It soon becomes apparent that the critical element is progress, not longevity. The question is not how much time we have logged, but how far we have progressed...." You see, my friends, life is not lineal, but experiential, not chronological but developmental. Time therefore has to do with "transitions," "realignment," and "development." It has to do with our capacity to identify and constantly execute appropriate course corrections to the end that we arrive at appropriate calculated destinations.

The Law of the Clock

The Law of the Clock is simply that time passes constantly, consistently, and absolutely. Once a minute has gone, it is gone! We can never retrieve it, we can't save it, and we will never find it if we lose it. The hands of the Clock of Time simply pass. It's like any other law; it does not care! It fundamentally dictates that time is more perishable than delicate fruit or flower petals. Each second comes and it goes; it's here and then it's not. Time obviously passes with or without a clock. It cannot be frozen, reversed, or accelerated. Time passes quietly, constantly, and without interruption.

A few years ago, I was en route to conduct a seminar in Kansas City when I sat by a gentleman who I learned was a Harvard Business Professor. As we discussed his role in the Harvard Business School, he shared an important concept. Although his commentary was pointed more toward college students, the message of his dialogue can be instructional to us all. He stated his opinion that much of what is taught in the college and university experience is masked in producing an even greater and more important premium. He said "if we could just teach college students that we are not only teaching them professional skills but more importantly we are first coaching and ultimately testing their capacity to live and manage their lives. College life is a mirror or reflection of life." Think about that for just a moment. "College life is a mirror or reflection of life."

As he continued a quantitative explanation of his theory, he invited me to consider these things. The average college student spends five thousand dollars per semester in tuition, books, food, clothing, social life, entertainment, travel, and so on. The traditional goal is to complete the college bachelor's degree experience in four years, usually in eight semesters. Therefore mathematically, students will spend about forty dollars every time they go to a sixty minute class. In fact, they spend forty dollars for every class they miss or sleep through. They spend forty dollars whether they are there or not, whether they gain any insight or not, or whether they enjoy the class or not. Business and employers then are given a "mirror-image" of what to expect and look for in prospective employees. They are able to see how students (candidates for employment) spend their own money at forty dollars per hour before they engage them in employment and spend forty dollars, fifty dollars, or even one hundred dollars per hour in wages and benefits. He summarized "employers can look at a student and ask, did the student spend their investment in themselves wisely? Did they attend class and therefore will they come to work or be an absenteeism risk in the workplace? Did they join clubs and get involved in outside activities and therefore will they be a positive image of the hiring company in their social life? Are they committed to important things or did they squander time on aimless socializing and mindless activity?

I am always interested to observe in my college teaching experience and as a father of high school students that far too many young adults go through their educational experience trying to determine how many times they can miss class and not be penalized, how they can get easy teachers, or what the minimum requirements for some grade will be. Why would anyone want to spend $40 to sleep through a class or sit idle in the popular gathering place for students during class time instead of attending class? It demonstrates to future employers they are an employment risk. It doesn't add up, does it? Spending money to exhibit non-performance. Showing others that we have little value for life and time. Remember, The Law of the Harvest eliminates our opportunity to cram. We can fake it for awhile, but long term we will demonstrate how we expended our effort and resources. If we sluffed, we will ultimately show our lack of capacity to perform long term.

We can all learn a lesson from this Harvard Professor. Remember, Time is a standard or measurement through which we can measure the progression or digression of self or group. How we spend or invest our time will ultimately impact our progression or digression. The Law of the Clock dictates that time passes consistently and constantly without interruption. How we spend our time tells a great deal about us, doesn't it? Getting control of the events in our lives does a great deal to position us for moving our lives toward progressive living.

The Law of Opportunity

The Law of Opportunity is that life produces more to do than time to do it in. There are always more things to engage in, participate in, and be involved in than time to do them in. Can you relate to this law? Once a seminar participant raised his hand and challenged this law, "what about when there actually is nothing to do? If I am stranded on a desert island waiting to die, there's not much to do. If laws are universal then I am not sure this one is a law because sometimes there really isn't anything to do." Before I could respond, a thoughtful college-aged participant disputed his older and wiser counterpart's provocation with a list of three or four things he could do on a desert island and then assured us all that waiting to die was only one option and one he personally would not choose to engage in. I invited everyone to join me in building a list of opportunities or activities a person could engage in while on a desert island. We listed over twenty possible legitimate activities in which we could engage ourselves, not to mention another twenty which were a little crazy. We could think, write in the sand, dig a well, take a walk, consider the future, cry, exercise, sleep, sing, pray, find beauty in the sunrise and sunset, create a poem, memorize, study sand crabs, comb the water for edible sea life, and the list could go on and on. The challenger resigned his protest with an important understanding. Opportunity is limited only by our mind and that choosing to do nothing is really choosing to do something. Nothing is something! Choosing to do nothing is a choice which may be an appropriate priority when considering the other options. However we still choose. The Law of Opportunity clearly asserts that life will produce, create, and offer more alternatives to which we can direct our attention than we have the capacity to focus on.

The Art of Discretion

The Laws of the Clock and Opportunity give us a chance to learn and perfect the Art of Discretion. Human beings are different than other animals in one major area. Most animals live more by instinct and apparently have little capacity to consider options and make choices. Human Beings can. We can think and determine, to some extent, how the choices we make will effect us. We choose to go to class, to work, or to church. We choose to sleep, study, or work out at the local fitness center. We choose to telephone an old friend just to chat, to visit an elderly relative, or to take our child to the zoo. We don't have to do anything! We choose to. While we will develop this idea more completely later, it is important for us to recognize that the Art of Discretion is a vital element in the consideration of Time. Like other Arts, it is learnable. My own experience teaches me that it is also very forgettable! Conscious effort is required to maintain and sharpen The Art of Discretion. I can forget how to say "No." This art is one that requires relentless determination to understand value, priority, and importance. To choose means to say "yes" to truly important things and "no" to those things which are not. Goethe once said "Things which matter most must never be at the mercy of things which matter least." The Art of Discretion, then, requires judgment and the capacity to discriminate. The definition of "discretion" helps us to understand the Art more completely. Discretion is the capacity to discriminate or employ the power to discern value; the power to judge or act; the act of being selective or discreet. The Art of Discretion is to think, focus, and identify those activities and issues which have the most value. The Art then, requires judgment and capacity to discriminate between Vital and Urgent things in our lives.

Let's take a look at these two words and ascertain their basic meaning:

1. Urgent—that which calls for haste, immediate action, or application of pressure. Urgent issues are things which must be done or else! They tend to be crises, pressing problems, deadline-driven assignments, or last minute preparations. It is important to understand that many "urgent" matters become urgent due to procrastination or lack of planning and preparation. In other words, while many urgent concerns raise their shrieking heads without warning and are completely beyond our control, many or maybe even most are created by us. Urgencies scream for and usually get our attention by saying "DO ME NOW, DO ME NOW, DO ME NOW" over and over again.

2. Vital—that which has great meaning, significance, worth, conesquence, influence, or value. It is essential, requisite, or extremely important. Important concerns usually deal with preparation, pre vention, planning, relationship building, and creation of ideas or personal insights. Doing "Vital" things inspires and increases confi dence and therefore courage. Doing the Vital things tend to increase quality in our lives.

With these definitions in place, let's look at Time and Life Management more closely. Since the early sixties when we watched the first orbital space flight around the earth, I have been intrigued by rockets. This fascination has prompted me to ask, how does it happen? How can a cylinder of metal pointed in an upward direction find the power to lift itself against the tremendous pull of gravity and eventually hurl itself beyond the atmosphere into a state of weightlessness and freedom to move about almost effortlessly?

My cursory study of this question later in my high school years answered my inquiry with an understanding of a basic law of motion, discovered nearly four hundred years ago by Sir Isaac Newton. This law states that for every ACTION, there is an equal and opposite REACTION. Newton's law then explains why the air from a balloon propels the balloon in flight. A rocket burns fuel inside its cylinder in a special combustion chamber, which presses out with equal force in all directions. When the ACTION of combustion is sufficient enough, it flows out the nozzle, or back of the rocket, with such force that the REACTION is the continuous thrust of the rocket away from the flow of exhaust.

Now, this is not a lesson in rocketry, payload, oxidizer agents, boosters, or multi-staging. Nor is it a discussion about aerodynamics, lift, camber, deflection, and drag. It is however a useful metaphor to illustrate how people, like rockets, if adequately engineered, can propel themselves from the pull and friction of gravity or negativity to a state where life can be directed with less effort and therefore move more accurately toward a given objective.

Just as the Rocket's movement and power to overcome gravity is contingent upon ACTION taking place in the combustion chamber, our movement to greater heights of living are also activated by what takes place in our Inner Vessels or Chambers. The Inner Victory hangs on ACTION within, and REACTION on the outside. Powerful lift in our lives come from our capacity to powerfully direct our ACTIONS. This essential capacity comes as we learn and employ the Art of Discretion in discerning the difference between the VITAL and URGENT. It comes when we are able to create a list of things we need to accomplish and then discriminate between those activities which are "Vital," and those which are "Urgent," and only act upon the Vital.

Prioritizing is a discrimination exercise that needs to take place almost constantly. Some urgent tasks or concerns are also vital. If your toddler son falls into the a swimming pool, then your ACTION to retrieve the child is both urgent and vital. However, there is a chance that the fact that your child fell into the pool in the first place is because you didn't take proper action to prevent it from happening. If you are in school, and the research paper is due tomorrow and you haven't started yet, I'd say it is rather urgent and even vital to your grade that you get it done. However, the urgency of spending all night researching and producing a "cram" paper is directly associated with failure to make vital micro-investments into the research paper, and more importantly, your education. If I suffer chest pain followed by a heart attack, it is both vital and urgent that I attend to my health. However, my heart attack may be associated with my lack of "discretion" in doing things to keep my heart healthy over the months and years before the heart stopped performing its function.

Therefore as we consider the Vital, the Urgent, Action, and Reaction, let's understand the basics truths which govern the causes and effects.

1. Urgencies are not necessarily Vital.

2. Urgencies will diminish to a great extent by paying consistent at-

tention to Vital concerns.

3. Urgencies are typically short-term concerns with long-term impact, while Vital issues tend to be long-term concerns with significant long-term impact.

4. Acting upon the Vital things in our lives takes constant checking and rechecking.

5. Urgencies distort the focus toward acting upon the Vital things.

It is important to understand that the real key to Time and Life Management lies in our doing whatever is necessary to insure that our ACTION is based on the VITAL and not, inappropriately, drowning in the URGENT. We must learn to discern and have the courage to ACT upon Vital things. ACTION in vital issues always produces a combustion and reaction within the Inner Vessel which increase our capacity to accelerate our personal progression.

You may be saying "OK, I agree! In fact I have always known that what you are saying is true ... what I want to know is HOW! Give me a recipe for the Art of Discretion ... tell me how to prioritize! Come on, I want to know how to do it!" Well, I have bad news and good news for you. First the bad news. I know there are many methods of prioritizing. I have embraced and taught them many hundreds of times to others. I have lived the last nearly 10,000 days of my life making lists and giving them levels of Priority. I personally use the "A=Vital, B=Important, C=Can wait" method. I have added the sequencing mechanism of giving numerical value to the A's , B's, and C's on my list. I am sure I have benefitted from this daily exercise. Even though there are these and other methods of scrutinizing our ACTION list, the bad news is, there is simply no recipe!

The good news is that you can and will succeed in developing the Art of Discrimination if you will daily and even hourly check and re-check where you are with the Vital concerns of your life and whether or not the real urgencies or the subtle ones are acting upon what's really important. Be a list maker of ACTION items which will take you forward in your life. Most importantly ask yourself constantly "is what I am doing right now the most important thing I can be doing to move me toward the important things of my life?" If they are not, then develop the courage to make quick course corrections. The homing missile rocket has the capacity to make critical in-flight course corrections which ultimately ensures it reaches its target. The good news is that you can too. It takes a constant awareness and willingness to obey the innate inner prompting which will keep you on course.

Why Time Management for Lives in Transition?

We know that successful people love life. We know that time is the "stuff" life is made of. I want to invite you to think about how you perceive time. Think deeply about where you are spending most of your time. A good way to start is to ask yourself to evaluate the last twenty-four hour cycle. Where did you spend your 1,440 minutes? In Vital or Urgent activities? Be honest and be careful as you think back. There may be a tendency for you to rationalize and support yourself in all the good reasons why something was Vital when really it was Urgent. After you have taken a close look at the last twenty-four hours, check yourself on the last week and if your memory serves you well move to the past month. If you are honest you will catch an important impression about where you need to spend more time. Transition, development, realignment, and transformation activity are all Vital Activity. Reading this book with the intent of improving your life is Vital. The whole purpose of creating a Creed Document or blueprint for your life is to keep you in Vital Concerns. It is very important for us to understand that we will never get completely away from spending time on Urgent matters. Unforeseen important events will always be a part of our lives. However, let's understand this: If we will spend more and more time in doing Vital activities, Urgent issues will shrink to a manageable size. Furthermore, Vital activities will empower you with more courage and quiet confidence. Doing Vital things is typically a "Private" battle. When you win the Vital "Inner or Private Victories," your capacity to fight and win your "Urgent Battles" is increased.

So where will you find the time to spend on Vital Activities? You just can't stop fighting the Urgent battles, can you? You must continue to spend the time necessary to fight them or they will kill you. Look carefully! If you are normal, you will find significant blocks of time eaten by mindless messing around. Remember, make yourself accountable by constantly asking if any of your actions or their offspring are really urgent or important enough to steal Vital time. Just turn off the TV! You can find more time! If you have a TV addiction or feel you can't miss escaping into the episodic intrigue of "TV Soaps, Sitcoms, and Talk Shows," then make a one-day, then a one-week commitment to yourself that your life is more important than spending it escaping into the television tube. If you will truly dedicate all your energy to more Vital Time concerns, I will promise you that what you feel after a few days or a week will be so empowering to your life that you will never go back to mindless time wasters and saboteurs of your happiness and success. You will also find that The Art of Discretion is sharpened to the extent that you'll seldom be deceived by Urgencies again. Your focus on Vital matters will produce such abundant rewards that your transitional, transformational, and developmental abilities will increase significantly. Try it!

Another Thought about Time

I have observed that Time is the great equalizer. People are inherently not equal in an intellectual or economic sense. We each have different capacities to think and process mentally. Some seem to be gifted and have some inherent capacity to think while others struggle with abstract thought. Each person in the human family has a different economic circumstance. Some are born wealthy or win lotteries and some are born into poverty and deprivation. The one thing that is given to all of us in equal doses is Time. Everyone has twenty-four hours each day, no more and no less. We all have all the time there is! We can utilize the great gift of time to place us on equal ground in managing our progress. If a person has a tough time with math, he or she can compensate by using time to improve mathematical skills. If I have less money that the rest, I can spend my time in hard work and industry and equalize myself with others in the financial sense.

In all cases, Time is a blessing and commodity that enables me to measure progress.

Before we conclude this chapter, let's summarize WHY the placement of this discussion about TIME is here in the early chapters of this book. Since TIME is "the stuff that life is made of," all of us would do well to evaluate where we are spending or investing it. We should demand an accountability of ourselves for how we currently spend the greatest amount of time. If we are to be more successful in the next chapter of our lives than we were in the last, it will likely have something to do with how we deal with this pivotal commodity.

Students will need to determine that they will live a lot of time in the Vital sector in preparing and being ready to exhibit their work. They will need to stay out of "cram time modes" to the end that they learn for the long term and at the same time exhibit to themselves and future employers they are dealing with the "Mirror" of life appropriately. Dealing with TIME properly will give confidence and courage to make good choices that maximize success.

Those in mid-life crisis or course correctional time frames will want to ask important questions about where they can find and shift more time to Vital activities. Remember, all course correction action is in the Vital Time. It is in these Vital Concerns that we find the insight and energy to enhance our change, transformation, and realignment. This wonderfully important but disdainfully Not Urgent activity is where all of us can discover who we are, where we are going, why we are going there, what we must do, and how we are going to make it happen.

In all cases HOW WE INVEST OUR TIME today is the passkey into the future. If we invest it wisely, we will receive an incredible return. Time is so important and foundational to this exercise, we will return again specifically to discussion of it several times before we conclude this book.

Chapter Four

BELIEF SYSTEMS AND A PHILOSOPHY OF LIFE

It is time to begin the process of building your Creed Document or blueprint for the most important life you will ever have an opportunity to design ... Yours! We will start with a fundamental concern called "philosophy of life." Everyone has a philosophy of life; however, few give conscious attention to it. Only a tiny portion of the Human Family understands or takes responsibility to identify what their philosophy is and the impact it can have upon how they live. You are one of those few. I invite your attention and commitment to engage in this opportunity to examine your life so that you will be more directed and successful in both your private victories and public battles. Your public victories (those visible) are always preceded by the quiet private victories in the mind and heart. This section will direct you to conduct an audit of your belief system, to determine where you will begin in your transitional effort.

What Is a Paradigm?

The word "Paradigm" has become a buzzword in most corporate circles over the past few years. Some may feel it has been overused or prostituted, but whether you have heard the word or not, I invite you to really understand it. The word originates in Greek, meaning model, theory, perception, assumption, or frame of reference. It is the way one sees the world.

When we realize that all behavior, attitude, and thought is dictated by our "Paradigms," then it will give us a proper place to begin our transition. Everything we do, think, feel, and experience is influenced by the way we see the world. Dr. Covey states: "Each of us tends to think we see things as they are, that we are objective. But this is not the case. We see the world, not as it is, but as we are—or, as we are conditioned to see it. When we open our mouths to describe what we see, we in effect describe ourselves, our perceptions, our paradigms. When other people disagree with us, we immediately think something is wrong with them but sincere, clearheaded people see things differently, each looking through the lens of experience." Think of it! We see everyday life, not as it really is, but as we are. If all behavior finds its root in the way we see the world then it follows that if our paradigms are not consistent with the way the world really is, then we will

---

Belief Systems and a Philosophy of Life **33**

do dumb things! We do dumb, stupid, or moronic things because we fail to base our lives on true paradigms or principles.

Robert F. Bennett, in his book *Gaining Control,* describes this concept in yet another way in his explanation of "The Belief Window." He teaches that in front of each one of us *is* a large window through which we see everything. Although it *is* only imaginary, it *is* very real. Not only do we see the world through it looking out, but we also use it to filter all data that comes to us. On the pane of this imaginary window we write the principles by which we live. All behavior *is* influenced by what principles we have written on the window.

For example, if we have written on our window that the earth is flat, then our behavior is influenced when we are navigating the sea. If our window has a principle of belief that Levi brand clothing is superior to Wrangler, then our behavior in the clothing store is influenced. If we have the principle on our window that we are ugly, then our behavior in social settings is regulated by that belief.

So where do these beliefs or principles come from? To really identify what's on our window or what our paradigms are, we need to look at where and what conditions existed when we formed them. When I was eleven years old I delivered newspapers. My particular route covered a significant area of town. An early landowner in the area with the surname "James" had divided his farm into smaller acreages and distributed them amongst his several children. This area of town was unofficially referred to as "Jamesville," having ten or fifteen family homes in a semi-rural mini farm setting. Part of my route included Jamesville. The most significant recollection I have of Jamesville was that the families loved dogs and each had one or two large "watchdog" type animals. There were collies, German shepherds, dobermans, and a bulldog. From the first day I delivered newspapers there, every single one of those dogs tormented and tortured me with an exhibition of growling, snapping, and chasing. One particularly large collie changed the way I saw Lassie on TV. His name was Flash. He growled, snapped, and once sunk his fangs into my leg. Every day, day after day, I would walk down the road into Jamesville dreading the responsibility to provide newspapers to this small percentage of my customers. My experience in Jamesville formulated principles for my Belief Window and established early paradigms for the way I see dogs, particularly large dogs.

You can likely predict my behavior, even after more than thirty years. Whenever I see a large confident German shepherd approaching me, what happens? My body tenses up. If I can I will choose alternate routes to walk, or sometimes I'll even stop and walk the other direction. My behavior and what happens inside of me are affected by the way I see big dogs, which is based on my paperboy experience with the dogs in Jamesville.

The belief window itself is neither good or bad, it just is. However, the principles on the window can either be correct or incorrect. We are going to take steps to evaluate what principles we have written on our belief windows that are influencing our behavior. We want to examine the way we look at the world. We want to determine if our "paradigms" are accurate and appropriate to the extent that they are helping us in our efforts to improve or change. There is nothing more fundamental in our transitional battles than our paradigms regarding our world and its challenges.

There is power in paradigms. Another way to see them is that they are the maps of the territory. They are not the territory. Paradigms are maps which explain the features of the territory. If they are correct, they provide an orientation to where we are and what we can do to move in the direction we desire. However, what if the map is wrong?

Dr. Covey shares a significant insight in his use of the "map" metaphor in his teachings. Since our family resided in a Detroit suburb I found this illustration even more meaningful. One of the main orientations to downtown Detroit is the river which connects Lake Huron to Lake Erie. Across Lake Michigan is Chicago, which has a similar orientation to the waterfront on its eastern edge. Suppose you wanted to arrive at a specific location in Chicago. A street map would be a great resource to help you get oriented and ultimately arrive at your destination. However, suppose through a printing error you really received a map of Detroit. The heading reads "Chicago Metropolitan Area" but the streets, waterfront, and layout is Detroit. Can you imagine the frustration and disappointment you would encounter in trying to find a certain location? Your effort to arrive at your destination would be significantly impeded by your map or paradigm, not by your attitude or desire. You may want very badly to get to a certain place, you may have a positive mental attitude, a Pollyanna approach to life, but it would be a miracle for you to get to your destination if you are relying on an incorrect map or paradigm of the way you see Chicago when using a Detroit city street map.

I suggest that our arrival at desired destinations in life is pivotal upon the map (paradigm) we carry of the territory. I am just as confident that our inability to find a specific destination in Chicago with a Detroit map, is extended into life's other arenas. How can we be successful in our approaches to find success in college, careers, marriage, and in finding happiness if we have the wrong map or paradigm? How can we experience success if we have screwed-up principles on our Belief Windows? The purpose of this book and the exercise associated with this important component of your Creed Document or blueprint is to both examine and develop correct paradigms or at least invite improvement through seeing things differently.

The Paradigm Shift

It is important that we understand that "paradigms" are entrenched deeply in our minds. First impressions or experiences are sometimes difficult to renegotiate in our minds. More than three decades ago, I had my first encounter with an experience you are likely to have had in some way as well. I was at a youth leadership conference where a young, insightful college professor addressed us. I remember the experience today because of the impact it had on my thinking at the time. Perhaps, in many ways, this book and my intense desire to assist others through transition is an indirect result of that weekend in the early 1970's. He was bald, dynamic in his approach, and powerfully influential. I enjoyed his introduction, his demeanor, and his approach. I guess you could say that I developed an instantaneous "trust" for the things he taught. I felt the things he taught were correct and good. He conducted an experiment using an overhead projector and three separate transparencies. He divided the room into two groups, having the first group shut their eyes. He asked the second group to look at and mentally devour the transparency he placed on the projector while the other group, of which I was a part, closed their eyes and waited. After twenty to thirty seconds he removed the transparency without my group seeing it, had the other group close their eyes, then placed a different transparency on the projector and gave us similar instruction to view and absorb our impression of what was on the screen. After a similar amount of time, he turned off the projector and invited us to collectively open our eyes. He asked us to maintain a vivid image of what we had seen on the screen while he talked about first impressions, paradigms, and related ideas for approximately sixty seconds. He then placed a third transparency on the projector, turned it on, and asked us to explain our individual impressions of what we were seeing to the large group. One girl described what she saw, peacefully and almost as if the question was overly simplistic. Then another individual voiced disagreement. Half of us were emphatically describing a young woman, while the other half argued that it was an old woman. Disagreement! Within minutes the more verbal people were loudly making their points while the quiet types sat and wondered what was going on. As the discussion ensued, you could hear individuals in each of the smaller groups say "Oh yeah, I see it too," or "I see it" followed by a short chuckle. "Far-out!" someone would say in late 60s jargon.

There are two points I wish to make with this experience: First, we need to understand what we mean when we speak of a "Paradigm Shift." When we move to the point where we see something different than our original perception in an experience, that's a paradigm shift. We see the composite picture differently than we did previously. In the case of the aforementioned example, we can see both the old woman and the young woman interchangeably by shifting our mental view. Thomas Kuhn, in his instructive book *The Structure of Scientific Solutions,* shows how almost every major scientific breakthrough comes with the notion of a "paradigm shift," when there is a break or shift from old ways of thinking or old paradigms. Using Bennett's language of the "Belief Window," it is when we see the world entirely different as a result of placing a different "Principle" on the window. Similarly, if we are in Chicago and change from the map of Detroit to one of Chicago, then everything begins to make sense and frustration is reduced because we understand differently.

Secondly, I want you to know that even decades later, when I look at the pictures I see the very same impression of what I absorbed in those first thirty seconds in the late 60s. Paradigm shifts are sometimes hard to execute. The level of trust I had in this young dynamic professor who stood teaching a group of young adults in my northwestern New Mexico home town, together with the first intense review of the picture of the young woman, caused me to carry that first impression for much of the balance of my life. Yes, I can shift intermittently between the two, but I naturally gravitate to my first impression. That is often true in our maps, principles on the belief window, and paradigmatic consideration. We often stick to our first impressions and shifting takes work and time. However, if we will remember that all significant change and growth happens when we break away from old or erroneous paradigms based on incomplete information, our capacity to improve in our transitions is maximized.

Another paradigmatic concept worthy of brief mention is that of "Reframing." "Reframing" is to take a picture and reframe it so that it looks different. There is a person in my life, my older sister, who had an encounter with polio. Polio had a devastating impact upon what she could and mostly could not do. Her nature was to be extremely active and athletic, but in the aftermath of her bout with the dreaded disease, she could barely lift her head from her pillow. At first she was bitter, frustrated, and unable to deal with the realities of what polio had done to her. Then somehow a reframing took place; she determined that life had treated her as fairly as the next person. In fact, life had given her a "perspective" that could actually enhance her capacity to influence others in quiet, private, and wonderful ways. For nearly fifty years she has inspired and impressed hundreds of people to live life more focused and appreciative. She determined that her adversity was a part of the happiness she would experience in her life. We can all identify such an example. Someone who has developed the "art" of reframing. If someone comes to your mind at this time, go to Chapter Thirteen and jot that person's name down in the margin. You may want to use it when we develop another section of your Creed Document.

As we examine our Belief Windows or maps, let's do so with an eye to identifying whether or not they are correct and are delivering the kinds of outcomes to our lives that are consistent with what we really want and deserve. Paradigm Shifts are necessary to transition. Significant change and transformation into a better life cannot be executed by the same level of thought or perspective we had when we created our past life. On the assumption that we want to improve and become better in the next new chapter of our lives than we were in the previous one(s), we must shift to a higher or more correct level of thinking and seeing. In some cases we may need to take our picture of life to the frame shop for a major reframing. If we want to make quantum sustained changes and improvements, we have to focus on changing our paradigms, not our behavior.

The Law of Belief

This law states that our behavior and actions are consistent with our paradigms and beliefs. Again, laws don't care, they just are! Remember, belief is the foundation of all behavior. Beliefs are conclusions we have formed based on our experiences or sometimes on the experiences of others who we trust. Beliefs are the roots of all outcomes.

The Art of Belief Inspection

Being able to carefully inspect our paradigms is both important and learnable. Let's practice by looking at how some paradigms have changed the world of others.

Years ago, it was the paradigm of doctors and human physiologists that it was impossible for a human being to run a mile faster than four minutes. It was a shared paradigm that the demands upon the human body to run a mile any faster than four minutes would cause the heart to explode. Therefore, the paradigm produced hundreds of years of running times many seconds over four minutes. One day, however, Roger Bannister broke the four minute mile and his heart did not explode. Today, athletes in world competition finish many seconds under four minutes. In fact, we are witnessing performances nearly a third of a minute under four minutes. How can that happen? Is it Nike, Reebok, or Avia shoes? Is it in the genetics? Is it in the food runners eat? I don't think so. The paradigm was revisited, the old belief examined and changed. The result is evidenced by the many who run at high schools, colleges, and professionally under the four minute mark.

Similarly, in the game of basketball, years ago it was a rarity to ever see a player under six foot who could dunk the basketball. "Dunking" (slamming or jamming) the basketball requires that the player elevate himself sufficiently to take a regulation size ball in his hands with outstretched arms above a ten foot rim and push the ball down through the hoop. For players nearly seven and one-half feet tall like Shaquille O'Neal or even six and a half foot players like LeBron James, the task is not significant. But for those whose height or leg strength is not their forte, the feat of "dunking" was reserved for the big guys since it was impossible for little guys to elevate themselves sufficiently. That is until someone forgot to tell pint-sized Spud Webb who only approaches five and a half feet that little guys can't dunk! As one of the smallest players in the NBA, he won the NBA Slam Dunk contest in the early 1980s. A paradigm shift occurred. Young players were no longer limited by the belief that little guys can't dunk. While living in Detroit in the winter of 1988, I accompanied my son to his games in an inner city basketball league for seventh graders. In just a few years the Spud Webb paradigm shift had produced some incredible fruit. I observed with my own eyes, little guys, young little guys twelve and thirteen years old whose height was in the five and a half foot range, slamming, jamming, and dunking the basketball with unbelievable authority. It was at first unbelievable to me because my paradigm had not previously really shifted. I must have thought "Spud is a freak, he's really unusual, he's worked hard to overcome his shortness, he's one guy we'll remember as overcoming his height barrier, it'll never happen again, etc." That Saturday morning in downtown Detroit completed the shift. I now believe! Recently in 2006 another small player Nate Robinson 'wowed' the crowds as he won the NBA Slam Dunk Fest @ 5'9".

I have used sports-related examples, but the evidence is seen in all arenas of life. The sports world is constantly keeping score, measuring, monitoring, and is built around determining performance against performance. We find it easier to look to athletics as a source to provide examples of those things where new levels of performance are achieved.

Let's look at other examples where we can hone our skills in examining and inspecting limiting beliefs or incomplete paradigms. Not long ago, a young man asked if he could visit with me about his career plans. As we talked, he shared with me a great level of frustration with his father and three older brothers. He came from a multigeneration agricultural family that made its living doing custom farming for land-owning farmers. They owned no property of their own but contracted with land-owning farmers to prepare the soil, fertilize, and then harvest the crop for a percentage of the profit. While the family operation was only marginally successful, it did provide for the needs of several families. As this young man became of age, he desired to attend college and follow different professional pursuits as an accountant. He said to me, "My older brothers constantly remind me that the professions are for other people, smart people, and people who have money ... Grandpa was a custom farmer and built a good business, Dad took it and now it is up to us to prepare to take it." He continued, "Every time the subject revolves to education Dad says, `Bill, don't go to college! For you, its a waste, we already have our lives cut out for us, and besides we need you here."

What's the paradigm? What does the family have written on their belief window? What can you predict about what paradigms or principles dominate in the life of my young friend? What will be some of Bill's greatest challenges in his upcoming transitions of whether or not to attend college or stay in the family business? How will his present paradigm influence the balance of his life? Unless there is a significant stimulus for them to leave custom farming, the father and brothers will likely never make a change. Chances are very good that in the next generation their sons will carry on the family tradition and business. Their paradigm of how they are to make a living is fixed. Bill's greatest challenge will be to break out of the paradigm that the "professions" are for other people. Perhaps he only needs to reframe his view of the custom farming business. When his education gets hard, the cost of tuition and books get high, and things at university get tough, the paradigm created and passed through two generations will surface again to his belief window. If we were able to listen to his internal dialogue, chances are good we would hear him say to himself, "maybe they're right! All the CPAs I know are rich, and I just don't know if I'm cut out to be rich. I'm so darn poor right now ... maybe I should just go back and join them in the family farming operation ... it really isn't a bad way to make a living." He will have to part with and replace the old paradigm or his transition will be short, incomplete, and certainly not developmental, transformational, or realigning.

Bill asked me for reassurance when he said, "What do you think? Should I go to college or should I stay here with the family business?" My response was "Yes." He said "Yes, what?" I responded again by saying "Yes." A little perplexed, he said "I don't think I understand."

What's driving his desire to not follow the same career path that his grandfather, father, and three older brothers have chosen to follow? What's driving the paradigm? Maybe it's money—perhaps he feels he can make more money in his professional life? Maybe his paradigm includes the idea that he's different than his father and brothers. Or maybe there is something on his window from his experience that verifies he loves numbers, calculation, and working with financial analysis problems. Or maybe the paradigm of the custom farm business is that he hates dirt, long hours, and working for his dad. We don't know, do we? So what advice would you give him about inspecting and carefully examining his belief or paradigms associated with this issue? What would you say?

I said "Yes! Go to college and get a degree in accounting and become a CPA or stay home and get into the family business." He looked at me as though he was viewing a complete idiot. I then told him that I knew a custom farming operation in another state where the owners were actually some of the wealthiest people I knew. His response gave me a clue to what was fueling his paradigm. He did not say "so what" or "big deal" or "I love accounting." He said "you do?" I told him of how the custom farmer I knew (who was now about his father's age) had taken his father's fledgling business fifteen years earlier and built a service reputation second to none. He expanded his capacity to give incredible service to those with whom he contracted and over time, he had increased his income many times over. Incidentally, I also told Bill that this man had graduated from a great agricultural university in the west. When I told him that, his reaction gave me a hint of his paradigm. He looked at me this time with a sparkle in his eye and said, "I've always liked what we do, but it never occurred to me that I could make any money at it." Can you see what the inspection did? I provided him with a more complete view of his own paradigm by looking at the results created by someone else who had a more complete perspective of custom farming. Most of the time, since paradigms stem from our own experience, they are not incorrect, they are just incomplete.

If we were to inspect the paradigmatic metamorphosis of how a Roger Bannister or Spud Webb saw their world, we would likely observe that they too had to change the way they saw things relating to their respective sport. Roger, Spud, and my young friend Bill had to change their level of thinking, their view of the world, and their beliefs before they could be empowered to change, transform, develop, and realign.

Before we move on, maybe we could ask about the paradigm of the wealthy custom farmer. 'What was his paradigm of custom farming or what principle was clear on his window that was different from that of Bill's or perhaps even Bill's family? His capacity to create wealth was prefaced by his view of what was possible, wasn't it? Maybe it would be good to look at the paradigm or view of the world as seen by Bill's father. I don't want to suggest that his paradigm was incomplete or inadequate. His view may have included feelings or beliefs about how family farming or the business taught wonderful character traits of hard work, industry, and unity. His view or beliefs were probably just as noble and good as the wealthy custom farmer's, but they were different. The important thing to remember is that the behavior of both was a function of their beliefs. Our behavior, the things we do, is always rooted in the way we see our world. Our actions, emotions, and attitudes are fundamentally influenced by our paradigms.

One more example: Several years ago a friend came to-me and informed me that he felt he was going to divorce his wife of twenty-three years. He said, "Things are not the same anymore. I just don't love her." He went on to explain how the fire of their romance was no longer burning. He clarified that while there was no fighting nor disagreement between them, the feeling of love and caring was gone and that he felt he wanted to divorce her. I asked him if his spouse felt the same way. He said "No, I have not even told her that I want a divorce but she would be stupid if she can't feel that we've fallen out of love." After sharing a lengthy explanation of his justification for leaving his spouse and assuring me that he was not seeing nor was interested in any other woman at that time, he asked, "So what do you think I should do?" I responded "You've just told me what you're going to do. I'm confused that you're asking me for an opinion of what you should do." He quietly looked back at me. I continued, "I care for both you and your spouse and want the best for both. Do you really want my opinion?" With head bowed looking at his feet he said "You know I do, that's why we're here together talking and that's why I am sharing my feelings with you."

"Let me see if I understand," I said. "You don't love her anymore. You don't feel anything for her anymore. You don't do anything anymore with her ... is that right?"

"Yes, that's it," he responded. "Have you ever considered that maybe that's the whole problem?" I said. "I'm not sure I understand what you mean," he said.

"Love is as much a verb as it is a noun, if not more," I said. "Feel" and "do" are first-class verbs. Verbs are action words. If you want to know what I think, I think you should Love Her, I think you should Feel, and I think you should get off your backside and go love her. Buy her flowers, take her for a ride or a walk, send her a love-letter through the mail, do, do, and do things that show an active love for her," I counseled. He looked me in the eye and I knew we had somehow connected. I hesitated and then gave him one last thought, "You fall into mud, you fall into cow pies, you fall out of bed, you fall down and skin your knee but you don't fall into love ... you work at it. When you knew you loved her twenty-three years ago you paid a lot of attention to her. You took her to the movies, you held her hand, you touched her gently, you hugged her, you took her to dinner, you were busy doing many things to court her and let her know you loved her, didn't you?" I said. He nodded affirmatively. "Go love her!" I suggested. He did. That was nearly tthirty years ago. They are still married and as near as I can tell they are best friends. They are loving (the verb) each other.

Let's ask ourselves a few questions about my friend's beliefs and paradigms. What was his paradigm of "love"? What was his view of the solution to the loss of it? He was so stuck on the notion that it was a thing you feel, and not a thing you do, that his behavior was to sit around and wait for it to touch his heart. Love is a verb. It is one of the most important verbs we will ever know and seek to understand. Our understanding and examination of how our paradigm affects our behavior in doing something about it is critical to "transition, change, development, transformation, and realignment."

As you consider your transitions, it is always- important to reexamine your Belief Window. New environments almost always dictate critical inspection of pivotal paradigms.

I love to travel and have a special feeling for Meso-America (Mexico, Guatemala, and Central America). If I were to transport a Guatemalan farmer from his beautiful highlands with an agricultural paradigm in a land which is called the "eternal spring" to a farm in Iowa, he would have to make some real adjustments to his thinking. His paradigms would have to be examined and adjusted from triple or even quadruple planting seasons each year to one critical season. His view of soil preparation, water, and harvest would have to change if he were to experience any success at all. Likewise, we must take a good hard look at the way we see things and determine if they are environmentally accurate.

When a person leaves the structure of high school and attends college, like the farmer, he or she must examine his or her belief windows and paradigms, adjusting to meet the environmental changes, in order to reap the harvest desired. Adapting to a new life will be only as successful as our ability to check paradigms and appropriately conform.

Weddings, university graduations, employment transfers and promotions, and mid-life are great times to reexamine the paradigms. How many people do you know who can pull from their bookshelf or prominent place on their personal desk, a blueprint or creed document that outlines and discusses critical paradigms of their lives? Not many, I'll wager. Like a blueprint in building a house, if you have a Creed Document to frequently review and consult, I promise you and even guarantee that your life will be better and your transitions will be more smoothly executed.

ASSIGNMENT

This is the first of several invitations extended to you to create your Creed Document or life's blueprint. Obviously, whether or not you do anything with the invitation is entirely up to you. I want you to know that thousands of lives have been enhanced by the process and the results. Give it a try!

---

1. Select several (maybe six to ten for a starter) issues or principles that you feel are critical to your life. They ought to be things you feel strongly or passionately about. Maybe a couple of them ought to be beliefs which you feel are or will be critical in your immediate or upcoming transitions. Make a short list of these concerns.

2. Take each issue and write down what your philosophy is about it. Express in writing your view or paradigm of what is important about each. You may find it an interesting experience. Do you know what you really believe? As you work at identifying your beliefs talk to others about them if you like. Write your feelings down.

One person entitled this part of the Creed Document, "My Ten Articles of Belief," another calls it "Preamble Paradigms." You may entitle yours whatever you want. If you will engage in this invitation, you will find that your beliefs about critical issues become very clear and concise. You will begin to sense an empowerment process well up inside of you. You will find that more often your behavior and actions are clearly more immediate and focused because your paradigms are more explicit, your belief window more clear, and your principles more powerful.

What are your beliefs? For a starter, what do you feel about some of the words below? How would you define them? Select three or four and express your definitions or paradigms according to your personal experiences. How do your maps define them?

Adversity	Testing	Experience
Honesty	Education	Travel
Health	Home	Reading
Family	Life	Fun
Leadership	Death	Spontaneity
Success	Failure	Parenthood
Intimacy	Love	Music
Sex	Money	Science
Maturity	Career	Media
Friendship	Marriage	Punishment
Improvement	Challenge	War
Development	Change	Crime
Time	Work	Forgiveness
Destiny	Loyalty	Winning
Self-Esteem	Growth	Possessions

The most important issues may not be on this page. Remember, think of things that you feel are important as you live your life now and in the future. As you develop your philosophy statement about each, answer questions like: What's the definition of this? Why is it important to me? What does it look like or how can I tell when I see it? Why will this make a difference in my actions? Is this really important to me in the long term?

Tell someone else how you feel about it. Telling someone else at this point is not so much to get their opinion as it is to hear yourself articulating it. Sometimes, I have found that in telling someone else, hearing it aloud from my own mouth helps me clear up or even detach from some element of the idea that really isn't all that important after all. Other times, just articulating and telling someone else has ignited a passion for the thing I'm talking about. Telling others is a clarifying activity.

This will not take long, so do it! The important steps are:

1. Selecting a few issues or ideas.

2. Discussing them with others as appropriate.

3. Writing them down.

4. Telling others what you wrote or believe.

5. Refining (over time).

Example 1

MY PHILOSOPHY OF LIFE

I believe:

1. Adversity is a prologue to discovery ... of finding out what I am and whether I can find wisdom in my experience.

2. Money is a source of power. It can build good or it can create bad. The love of it can ruin all that matters. Not enough of it can destroy. Too much of it can develop weakness of character. The want of more of it can make those who pursue it miss more important things. Accumulating it at the expense of sharing it makes it valueless.

3. Failure is fertilizer. It makes men and women grow.

4. Success is gaining a capacity to enjoy living.

5. Time is a standard by which we measure progression or digression.

6. xxxxxxxxxxxxxxxxxxxxxxxxxxxxxxxxxxxxxxxxxxxxxxxxxxxxxxxxxxxx
   xxxxxxxxxxxxxxxxxxxxxxxxxxxxxxxxxxxxxxxxxxxxxxxxxxxxxxxxx

7. xxxxxxxxxxxxxxxxxxxxxxxxxxxxxxxxxxxxxxxxxxxxxxxxxxxxxxxxxxxx
   xxxxxxxxxxxxxxxxxxxxxxxxxxxxxxxxxxxxxxxxxxxxxxxxxxxxxxxxxx

Example 2

THIS I BELIEVE . . .

That life is my greatest gift. What I do with it and how much of it I give away will be my gift back to its creator.

That intimacy is sweet. It is stirring but never out of control. It is caring for the outcomes in the other persons life more than my own. It is gentle, never abusive. It is reserved, never exploited.

That education is lifelong. It is the key to open doors of possibility. It is learning to use wisdom.

My career should be first enjoyed and then compensated. I should enjoy doing what I do and my performance should be the best I have to offer. My compensation in part is the enjoyment of knowing I do what I do well and that it somehow makes a difference.

Chapter Five

HARNESSING THE POWER OF MENTORSHIP

Several years ago I had an experience in the Canadian wilderness that has had a significant impact on my life. About twelve boys, fifteen and sixteen years of age, traveled by bus with three adult leaders to Ely, Minnesota. When we arrived at a canoe base, we were outfitted and oriented by a young man in his mid-twenties who was to be our guide for the next ten days. He taught us how to navigate a canoe, demonstrated how to swamp a canoe, and demonstrated what we should do in several emergency situations. Using a map, he showed us the direction we would go into the wilderness and educated us about scanning the edge of a lake or stream to find intermediate destinations called "portage trails" which connected the lakes and rivers we would be navigating.

Over the next few days we became very confident in our ability to both navigate the wilderness waterways and propel our canoes. He praised us and told us that our group was one of the strongest groups he had ever directed. We even got a day ahead of the original schedule because we were able to travel faster than the normal pace with groups our size.

One day, as we stopped by the edge of a slow moving river, he asked us to stop and receive instructions. We had already identified our destination across the river ... a portage trail about a hundred yards downstream. He said, "Gentlemen, I want you to listen to me very closely. This river is very deceiving, as you look at it, it seems to be moving very slowly. But in order for you to get across the river you must point your canoes at a forty-five degree angle upstream and use every bit of power you have to get across the river and catch that portage trail. Place your power man, the strongest paddler in the front of the canoe and go like h_, or you won't make it across." As I recall, we listened but did not comprehend the impact of what he was instructing. After all, we were the strongest group he had ever taken into the outback of this beautiful wilderness. We were strong, invincible youth, made confident by our four days of extraordinary performance. However, he was a seasoned wilderness guide, enlightened by his own experience and by the wisdom of sage frontiersmen who had come to know the hazards of the waterways.

Sensing our overconfidence, he quietly enjoined us to listen anew, "Listen!" he invited, "what do you hear?" We listened and could hear the birds, an occasional call of a loon in the distance. "Do you hear that?" he questioned. We responded by telling him we heard the birds, the loon's call, and the wind whispering through the pines. "No, listen more closely," he insisted. Again we pointed our ears and attention to the sounds of the Canadian Wilderness. This time we heard the water of the river splashing very gently against the rocks along the edge in front of us and the more faint sounds of flying insects. When we reported our newest findings, he shook his head and said something like "Gentlemen, if you listen to the sounds of the river, it can teach you about its delusionary snares. You must learn to listen." Still not understanding the impact of his message we poised ourselves to listen even more intently. We strained to hear more but could not until he said "Listen closely, can you hear the ever so faint sounds of distant thundering water? The sound blends so easily with all the other sounds that it is difficult to even hear it. Can you hear it?" First one and then the other identified the sound and assisted the rest to discover the distant clue of what followed this lazy moving water in front of us. "If you don't get across this river in a timely fashion, you will likely be unable to get out of the water before you hit a series of falls that can take your canoe and your life and wrap them both around a boulder. You will not survive. Do you understand?"

We had a new appreciation for what he was trying to explain to us. We had been taught and warned of impending danger. We had this advantage to help us avoid being sucked into a crisis situation which could have marred our delightful experience in the outback of the Canadian Wilderness. We had been mentored by someone who knew the river.

The power of mentorship is in understanding that others know "the river" better than we do. Others have been down the river and see it from the per-spective of experience. Others see the river not just as it is but what it be-comes. The person who understands and harnesses this power will avoid unnecessary failure and enhance his or her capacity to navigate through the rough spots, should it become necessary. It is apparent that successful people understand and use this principle daily.

The Law of Light

"Light" as defined by *Webster's New World Dictionary* gives some wonderful indication of what this law is. Light is mental illumination, knowledge, information, enlightenment or spiritual inspiration. Thesaural synonyms in observation, and intelligence. The Law of Light is stated in two powerful words: "Knowledge exists!" Information and understanding are available. We can understand and we can gain knowledge of things as they are. We can obtain insight and be enlightened on matters pertinent to our lives. We may need to conduct a lengthy search which spans hours, days, months, years, or even a lifetime. However, the Law of Light shouts that without exception Knowledge Exists! Enlightenment *is* accessible. Mental illumination is obtainable. Inspiration is ready.

Mentorship: A Key to Light

Yale University psychiatrist Daniel J. Levinson reports in his study *The Seasons of a Man's Life* (New York: Ballantine Books, 1978) that people who tend to be successful in life develop a dream during their adolescence that is idealized by a person who personifies that dream. They then go on to engage in a friendship or relationship with an older successful individual who encourages, nurtures, and supports them in their pursuit of that dream and ideal. Think of it, who would be better to help you navigate any river of life than a person who has already realized what you hope to achieve.

It is especially appropriate in our transitions when we are making choices to enhance positive change and be more successful in the tomorrow of our lives that we get out and talk to people about "the river" we are investigating. If we can learn to ask questions, listen with an open mind, and seek to discover without prejudice, we will increase our chances of enjoying and navigating the river more aptly. I will get more specific later in this chapter about transitional suggestions for your consideration.

The Art of Inquiry

Being able to tap into "Light" is an art. As with all arts or skills, they are learnable. We can learn how to access Light and Knowledge. The Art of Inquiry is learning the skill of asking questions. It *is* learning to investigate, search, and probe to find the necessary information upon which we can build our lives. It is an art of examination.

The Art of Inquiry is developed as we learn to ask appropriate questions and then listen for meanings. When we can learn to ask questions that give us clues, we can identify the knowledge which will move us closer to desired objectives in our lives. What would you do? What have you learned? How can I know what you know? When should I? Where can I prepare best? How did you come to know? Who else knows? Why is it important? As we ask these vital probing questions, if we want Light and Knowledge, we must listen with an intent to understand and look beyond the short answers for deeper or hidden meanings. It's an Art we can all learn how to exercise.

Now, let's consider three ideas of exercising mentorship processes. First, we will look at the process itself. Second, we will consider the idea of finding and engaging in a relationship with a specific mentor in your life. Third we will entertain an approach to mentorship which requires no appointment or formal rendezvous whatsoever and allows you to include virtually anyone in your mentorship circle. Fourth, we will discuss the energy that flows to our own life when we mentor and give others the benefit of our experience. Let's consider:

Mentorship

There have been occasions after I have introduced the concept of mentorship when students approached me saying, "I cannot identify anyone to be my mentor." I understand what they are saying. They are living by the assumption that the power of mentorship lies in our ability to find a specific person whom we can identify as our "coach," "advisor," or "trusted friend." While such a relationship is often desirable, it is only an application of the process. We don't need a specific person or trusted friend to be our mentor to apply this principle. Mentorship as a principle is more of an attitude. It is learning to ask questions about "the river" you wish to navigate of anyone and everyone who knows something about it. It is noting their responses so that you can begin to form your own opinions and chart strategies that will get you where you want to go. Do you understand? Having a specific mentor is only one application of the principle. Learning to seek out information is the principle.

Learn to ask good questions, especially about your transitional concerns. For example, when you talk to those you ascertain as qualified to give you insight, ask questions which begin like the following:

- How did you come to know ... ?

- Where did you find out about ... ?

- Why did you choose to ... ?

- What have you learned from your experience ... ?

- Who else would you suggest I talk to ... ?

- What can I read to help me...?

- What steps do I need to take to ... ?

- How can I develop the same skills or insights ... ?

- When do you think is the best time to ... ?

- What would you do over or change if you could ...

- What do you see for the future of ... ?

- Who or what should I avoid in my efforts to ... ?

- How much time do you think I should allocate to ... ?

- Here's an idea I've had—what do you think about this approach ... ?

- From your perspective, do you think that _is a good idea to ... ?

- If you could guide me through the same experience you had in arriving where you are today, what three things would you want me to observe when I ... ?

Your ability to learn to ask questions and note the responses is fundamental to the process of applying the principle of mentorship. These are searching, introspective, specific questions that prompt the person you are interviewing to identify answers that will help you make even better choices. During this process, if you can identify even one "waterfall in the river," which you hadn't understood existed, you will enjoy higher levels of performance and success in your life.

Identifying and Connecting with a Specific Mentor

The word mentor is defined by the dictionary as "a trusted, loyal counselor, a wise teacher, a coach, a tutor." In the "Karate Kid" movies, Mr. Miyagi could be identified as such a mentor. He sees both a need and a solution to young Daniel's life and sets about to teach him the skill and wisdom necessary for him to succeed both on the championship karate mat and in life itself. You may know and seek to invite a "Mr. Miyagi" into your life. If you do, understand that you must ultimately be "invited" by the person on their terms. You will need to be sensitive to their time and interests.

As you consider selecting such a person, think over the past years of your life. Do you know anyone who has unknowingly already played the role? Can you think of anyone else who has made similar mistakes to yours? Does anyone come to mind who has experienced a failure to which you can relate, wherein the person overcame the challenges of defeat to arrive in the winner's circle?

If you are a student moving into the transition of another dimension of your education, whom do you know who has been through the same transition? If they succeeded, ask them what they did and note their responses for consideration as you proceed into the same "water." If they failed, ask them questions which will help to identify the kinds of things you will want to avoid.

If you are transitioning through a mid-life crisis, identify a person who has encountered the same challenge and won. Develop a friendship and rela-tionship of trust with them. Share your situation with them and invite them to impart to you the wisdom they have gained in the process of working through and finding themselves. You will want to be careful and exercise caution on two counts:

> First, we're not all alike and certainly don't have identical situations. Look for principles learned and harnessed, not for specific plans of action or application. If you can identify the principles, they are universal and become self-evident. Stay away from recipes or check lists of exactly how to overcome your challenge. Otherwise, you may become frustrated in your attempt to apply the principles in the same way they did. Look for principles, not recipes.

> Second, be careful not to engage with a mentor who is experiencing the same challenges as you. You have heard the expression "Misery loves company." Many times, two or more miserable people find each other and commiserate until they find that they are not helping but hindering

one another. While you may be comforted by knowing others are having the same challenges or that you are not the only one struggling, spending time discussing or reviewing life's problems will usually make things worse. If you find yourself in the company of someone who is struggling with similar transitional concerns, be kind to them and be willing to share your perspectives. What you need is someone who is far enough ahead of you in his or her midlife battles to have found solutions which will inspire you to find yours. Be on the lookout for someone who will help you see more clearly and execute more definite solutions.

Board of Advisors

This is perhaps one of the most intriguing mentorship concepts to apply. For some, it is difficult, but for most it is not only useable but a powerful application that transcends transition. It is a way to apply the Law of Light through the Art of Inquiry that can empower your life in an incredible way.

It is based upon the notion of the advisory committee. We are all familiar with Boards of Directors, Advisory Boards, School or Education Boards, Planning and Zoning Boards, even a Jury. The power of a "Board" is that a group of people with different paradigms, maps, and perspectives collectively form one voice through a committee process. Perhaps you have been on a Board of some sort. Usually those participating on such committees are nominated, elected, selected, or invited based on the view that their perspective is valuable to the whole.

Periodically boards change as needs change or as levels of contribution decline. When the perspective of one of the members is no longer needed, the person is usually replaced by one who has a fresh viewpoint. Many times Boards are designed to include a "visiting chair" or one who will fill a temporary advisory capacity while certain issues are being addressed.

I am of the opinion that you and I are important. In fact we are extraordinarily important. If IBM is important enough to have a Board of Directors to guide its course, the president of a country significant enough to assemble his cabinet for advice, or an educational system substantial enough to elect a school board to direct its progress, then I know you and I are important enough to have the same. We obviously may lack the economic resources to hire a cadre of individuals to give us direct consultation regarding the direction of our lives, but we do have the discretion to assemble a group of people to mentor us and provide us with perspective as we seek enlightenment and knowledge about living.

If you could select anyone, absolutely anyone, to be on your Personal Board of Advisors, whom would you choose? Expand your mind to include anyone who has ever lived or who may not yet be alive. That's right, anyone! Whom would you select? Would you invite Gandhi, Abraham Lincoln, or C. S. Lewis? Would it be Lee Iacocca, Zig Ziglar, or Tom Hanks? We can invite anyone to participate in giving us counsel and advice. There are no limitations! None!

Your Personal Board of Advisors is imaginary but can become incredibly real. Your study and knowledge of their lives will almost bring them to your table to whisper specific insights that will make your life better. Their own lives and examples will energize you to maintain a focus and direction to your life that will be important to what you become.

In order to explain the concept, I will share with you my own application of this dimension of Mentorship, the Law of Light, and the Art of Inquiry. As you note in the diagram, I sit at the one end of the table and surround myself with those individuals I have selected as my mentors. Their mission in my life is to assist me in accessing knowledge and understanding to the end that I live my life more profitably or progressively.

Rachel

Rachel is a child. I have invited three children to my Board. Rachel is one of them. She is four years old and at times reminds me of her grandmother. She has dark eyes, a splash of freckles across her little face, she has an innocence about her that inspires me. She lives with a smile on her face and blamelessly approaches life with a love for living each day. While I have come to know her, I have not officially met her. She is unborn. Her position on my Board is to be a constant reminder that my day-to-day decisions do have an impact upon the life she will someday live on planet earth. She reminds me of the undeniable fact that the choices I make influence others. She teaches me that while much of the world lives with the lie that "it's my life and I will live it how I want, it affects only me," I must understand and live differently. My choices affect Rachel, her brothers and sisters, her cousins, her children, and her children's children. Rachel is my granddaughter. While I may never meet her on this planet, I will meet her cousins and others of my posterity. I am grateful for her and her contribution to the direction of my life. Many of my choices are affected by her presence on my board and in my life.

Child #2

This little fellow is the second child on my Board of Advisors. He is tall and skinny for his age. His round moon face shows he loves life but finds it all a little overwhelming at times. He is the sixth of nine children and has been labeled as the "shy" one. He knows me better than almost anyone on my Board. He knows my struggles and he knows my successful moments. He has been there when I have overcome and he's been there when I've fallen. He knows my heart. He knows every action, reaction, and feeling of my life. He is me! He reminds me that life is an unfolding set of books, each having 365 pages per volume, all of which I author. He helps me to focus on the page being written today while using the lessons I learned yesterday, last year, and when he (I) was six, twenty, and thirty-two. This little boy helps me access the wonderful lessons we've lived and learned. I love this little guy!

Joseph #1

Sitting at Child #2's right is a man who's name is Joseph. Although he lived centuries ago, his life and legacy give me the capacity to keep first things first. He was hated by his brothers, they even attempted to take his life. Ultimately seeing the potential of making a monetary profit, they sold him for twenty pieces of silver. He was carried as a slave to a far-off country. He was in a different culture and wondered if he'd ever return to see his family. Although in a new land where none knew who he was or about his past, HE KNEW WHO HE WAS AND EVERYTHING ABOUT HIS PAST. He knew that he had special abilities, important relationships, and divine responsibilities. He maintained his focus through mistreatment, false accusations, public humiliation, prison, and discouragement to become a solution to the future temporal challenges of nations. He reminds me about commitment, responsibility, and adversity. That I am who I am whether alone and in the dark or surrounded by masses and in the spotlight. His life and example often help me discover "Light" or knowledge about living.

Joseph #2

Sitting directly across the table from Joseph #1 is another Joseph-hero in my life. This Joseph found life difficult but purposeful. Although he lived nearly two centuries ago, his encounters with life have impressed me. He understood the difference between journeys and destinations. His powerful capacity to lead amidst opposition and maintain a vision of purpose was incredible. He reminds me of many things, but especially he prompts me to awareness with regards to the place of adversity in my life and maintaining an attitude of constancy. Adversity helps me to grow, to become stronger, and to expand. It helps me discover more about me, my relationships, and my beliefs. His life demonstrated from his early youth to his death that you must have vision beyond the immediate and act upon what you know to be right, regardless of public opinion. He teaches me that "right" always wins in the end.

Parley

Sitting to the right of Joseph 2 is a man named Parley. He was actually nominated to my Board by a friend who encouraged me to read Parley's autobiography. In so doing, I became enamored of his colorful life. What stands out most in my mind is his capacity to listen to and understand "inner whisperings" and to have the courage to act upon them. He reminds me to consult my own feelings, quiet inner whisperings, and intuitive inclinations. Somewhere deep inside us is an ability to understand what rings true, what is right, and what is wrong. Parley reminds me to study with my mind, analyze with my brain, and then listen to my heart ... then DO IT!

Devin

Sitting at the right of Parley and to my left, is a wonderful friend that represents much of what's really important to me. He has been on my board of advisors since he was under five years of age. He is currently a young adult. He may be replaced someday or take on a new role with my Board. There are days when I am tempted to terminate his inclusion on my Board but somehow he just continues to be there in simple but powerful majesty. He is my youngest child and son. He is no more special than my other children but his position on my Board of Advisors is very intentional. He represents the people in this life that are most important to me and how my daily actions of attentiveness to their needs are critical to their growth and development. The greatest impact he has upon me is his uncommon willingness to forgive, love, be loved, and be loyal. Also, he has a sense of believing. He will believe anything I tell him, because I am his father. He will act upon, champion, and exhibit leadership in his world based upon the paradigms I give him. Although he is growing older and is starting to shed the looks of a little boy, I somehow sense that one of the deep-rooted characteristics of this person is his "childlikeness." Perhaps it is a trait he will not lose. In many ways, I want to be more childlike. I wish to be more like him.

My Chairman

While this book is not intended to be a religious work, I am Christian and one might expect that I will include some Christian values. I hope this is neither offensive nor inappropriate to you. Look for the principle in the process, and avoid being caught up in whether or not we agree in philosophy. The Chairman of my Board is Jesus Christ, who sits in His proper place, at the head of the table. My study of Him, His teachings, and His example have an impact upon me and my actions which I am unable to completely and candidly express. His life and role in my life have empowered me beyond anything or anyone else. All insights, enlightenment, inspirations, and AHA's must be ratified by the Chairman of My Board. All attitudes, plans, goals, and efforts must be passed by His all-knowing eye. Your Chairman can be anyone who you feel qualifies as one who has the capacity to lead you, who has a clear Belief Window, and who can help you see without prejudice.

Putting the Board of Advisors into Practice

The Board of Advisor's application has been one of the most powerful in my life. I want you to know that it is neither a real form of communication nor a cosmic connection. Once a seminar participant became so enamored with the idea that she began to make an effort to have a literal connective apparition-like experience with people of the past whom she had placed on her Board. Needless to say, she missed the whole point. It has been my experience that zealots who become fanatical about almost any idea will miss the value of the idea itself. This is a simple exercise where we identify inspirational individuals whose experience and insight give a perspective to our lives in a way that increases our love for life and what it can bring to us. It is just a way to formalize a group of heroes or individuals who inspire you.

For example, periodically I will sit down and identify a concern or two I am struggling with. I love certain kinds of instrumental piano, violin and saxophone easy-listening music, which has rhythm that is about the rate of the adult human heartbeat. I will sit down, or sometimes even lie down on the sofa or in my bedroom where I can turn on my stereo and play my favorite music while I have time to think. I ask myself, "So what would Rachel tell me about my problem or concern?" In turn, taking a few minutes for each, I ask myself what would Child #2 tell me, Joseph #1, Joseph #2, Parley, and Devin. Finally, I ask myself what my Chairman would have me do given the insight I've received as I've thought about each of my Board members. I usually come away from the fifteen or twenty minute experience with a clearer perspective. Sometimes I will notice that the thing I was struggling with or wondering about has found its way to either a solution or often fades completely away and is not a problem any more. Another thing I notice is that while each person on my Board has a different perspective, as I consider what they would teach me about my concerns they are always in harmony. The counsel I feel they would give me comes from a different angle but there is agreement in how I should proceed. Do you understand? The process is a way to formalize your thinking and meditation. It does not take the place of prayer nor of our petitions to God, Allah, or another deity. It is not an experience to try to connect with the unseen world. It is simply a study of others and an attempt to know them well enough so that you can find in their lives inspiration for your own. It gives a more formal, vivid way to think about perspectives and solutions or to just be introspective about how to live our lives. I encourage you to try it.

Prayer

If you believe in God or sense that there is a higher source for inspiration and guidance to supplement our human understanding, then prayer is a form of harnessing the power of mentorship.

I do believe in God and have personally found great power and direction in my life through prayer. It is perhaps the greatest mentorship principle you will ever employ. As I seek guidance through prayer, I remember that being mentored by God, means that answers to my questions come frequently through other people, situations, and circumstances. All answers which come from God are attended by "peace". Not all answers are the ones I had hoped for nor come in the way which I expected, but there is always a sense of peace which accompanies God's loving response and tutoring.

I suggest that we remember "The Law of Light: Knowledge Exists!" Further, that the "Art of Inquiry" includes at least as much listening as asking. If prayer is a part of our lives, we need to understand that it is more than pleading, supplication, petitioning, imploring, or even giving thanks. It is also listening and being open to the flashes of ideas that will surely come to as a result of prayer. Mentorship is a two way process. Remember to listen!

Summary

However you decide to employ this principle is up to you. I am not going to tell you how to do it, I will tell you that you will do well to apply it. Become more aware of the "Law of Light: Knowledge Exists!" Our job is to find it. To learn to inquire and find knowledge is our goal. When we find and have knowledge, we have the power to live a more directed and courageous life. The power of mentorship is finding knowledge, real knowledge, to guide us through the rivers of life.

ASSIGNMENT

1. Identify a problem, question, or even hobby or project you are involved in right now. Maybe it's about school, classes, career tracks, parenthood, relationships, or how to rebuild a motor. Take a pencil and paper and jot down a few of the things that concern you about it.

2. Next identify a person who you believe knows something about your concern.

3. Pick up the telephone and call them, go see them, or write them a letter. Ask them questions like the ones mentioned under the Art of Inquiry section.

4. Summarize their comments on paper. This kind of data can become a part of your Creed Document. Depending on the nature of your concern, the information and feedback you get from others as you learn to ask questions will be important and applicable to you for a long time.

5. Begin to study and think about your internal Board of Advisors and who you would select to fill the various positions. I have seven spots. You can have three or twelve. It's up to you. Begin to identify the persons. This can become a part of your Creed Document as well.

6. Select some music or identify a quiet enjoyable spot where you can think about the insights that would be given by each of your Board members with respect to your challenges. Expect a peaceful and energizing experience.

My Personal Board of Advisors

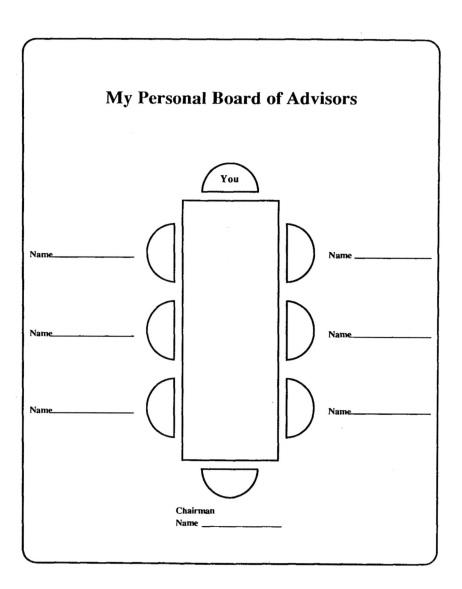

Chapter Six

UNDERSTANDING SELF AND OTHERS

In an earlier chapter, we discussed the concepts of paradigms and belief windows. We studied the Law of Belief which states that our behavior and actions are consistent with our paradigms or the way we see the world. Simply stated, belief is the foundation of all behavior. We determined that the skill of applying this important law is in the Art of Belief Inspection; stepping back to make a determination of what we really do believe.

In this chapter, we will study what I think to be the most fundamental contributor to our success. We will check, inspect, and carefully examine our paradigm of "ME" to determine precisely what we think about our individual self. This is unquestionably a vital link in producing the outcomes and results of our daily living. In many ways the answer to the question "How do you see yourself?" is the most important inner victory paradigm you will ever have. If we see ourselves as "unpleasant" to others, we will likely have a difficult time developing relationships. A person who sees himself as "average" in scholastic endeavor will likely never be on the Dean's List or receive the personal satisfaction of having a professor laud his performance. People who see themselves as "a klutz" in sports will seldom enjoy participating in them. How we see ourselves and how we feel about who or what we have the capacity to do, is central to the focus of this book concerning personal "transitions."

The Law of Uniqueness

As we seek to understand ourselves and view our capacity to become better at living, it is important to understand the Law of Uniqueness. When I think of uniqueness, I am reminded of a poem:

> Every blade of grass,
> And every flake of snow,
> Are just a wee bit different.
> There's no two alike, you know.
>
> For something small like grains of sand
> To each gigantic star,

Each one was made with this in mind
To be just what they are.

How foolish then to imitate,
How useless to pretend,
When each one of us come from a mind
Whose ideas never end.

There'll only be just one of me
To show what I can do.
And likewise you should feel very proud
There's only one of you.

Author Unknown

Isn't it interesting to consider that uniqueness is a fundamental law of the universe? Outside of identical twins, the makeup of the DNA molecule in every single person who has ever lived, now lives, or will yet live, is different from any other. Every single living person (billions of us) are different and unique. No two are alike. Every single snowflake that falls in the outback of Alaska to the New Zealand Alps, from Siberia to the Andes, and at the Park City Ski Area to Japan's famous alpine resorts, is unique and different. Therein lies a key to our enjoyment of who we are. Social systems have a propensity to dictate or shift us into being like each other. Advertising teaches us to be like the guy on the billboard or the model on the cover of our favorite magazine. Even our educational systems go unintentionally overboard to identify a model or standard for which every student must strive. While we need law and order to maintain and manage societal well-being, we somehow need to insure that it does not impede or snuff out the very nature of our being "unique." Each of us are born "different." Our differences in personality, style, perspective, and attitude are the magic which give us capacity to contribute and make our little corner of the world a better place. I invite you to understand unequivocally that each of us are uniquely good. Each of us exists to "sing our own song." The final chapter of this book will invite you to identify your song, the song you came to this planet to sing. Your song will be uniquely different but will harmonize with those sung by others to the benefit of at least one, (if not many) in the Human Family.

The Art of Sensing Individual Worth

Within days after birth, it seems our world began trying to teach us what we should do and how we should interact with other human beings. When we cried a loving adult picked us up, patted our back, and coaxed us with the words "don't cry." We were told it is was naughty to take toys away from other children ... that it wasn't nice to put fingers in our nose, or to jump on the sofa. We received hundreds of instructive edicts of what was right and what was wrong. "Don't talk too much," "be careful," "don't be so nosey," "you can't play," "you're too cautious," "day-dreamers are spacey," "you're so unappreciative," "get out of your rut and enjoy variety," "don't be so blunt," and the list goes on and on. While those making an effort to teach us probably had pure motives, we didn't have the maturity or power to understand their intent. We simply translated their instruction to mean, "There is something wrong with the way I am I must learn to be different." Year after year, we have been told "how to interact" and "what we should do." In fact, from about six years of age to eighteen, we received a barrage of do's and don'ts. One article suggests that the average grade school child receives over a hundred "Don't do that! It's not the right way. This is the way you're supposed to do it!" every school day before the morning recess. Please understand that I believe there are millions of wonderful teachers who attempt to teach and instruct with a desire to improve the world. However, since I am a teacher and a parent, I believe if I am not careful in the way I instruct or react, most of the time my messages will be interpreted as "Change yourself! There is something wrong or incomplete about the way you act, think, and do."

For the past several years I have had opportunity to interview hundreds of young people. I nearly always include a conversation and invitation which goes something like this:

> "It's great to visit with you today. I'm curious, as you think about your-self, what is the best thing about you? When others think of you, what do they think is the most positive trait about you?"

> (Silence)

> "It's O.K., it's just you and me here in the room, tell me the greatest thing about you. You don't need to feel awkward about being a brag-gart. What are the great things about you?"

"Well, hmmmmm! The best thing? I'm not really sure...." (Silence and reflective thought)

"OK, we'll come back to that in just a minute. Let's go to a question with a little different twist. From your experience, what do you think others would say are your greatest liabilities or the things you should work hard to overcome?"

(Very short pause) and then the person lists four or five things they could do to improve. "I shouldn't _____ ," "I am too   ," or "I can't

Why is so easy to enumerate our deficiencies and liabilities? Why is it difficult to create a list of great characteristics about ourselves that we are pleased with? I don't believe it has much to do with modesty or humility. I am coming to believe it has much more to do with the fact that our social mirror is constantly telling us we need to change.

It, therefore, becomes a challenge to develop the Art of Sensing Individual Worth. Each of us would do well to develop the practice of identifying and writing down good things about ourselves. The list should be reviewed often in order to counteract the waves of negative reminders telling us something is wrong with our uniqueness.

Developing the habit of "being glad we are who we are" is a habit worthy of our attention. In a later chapter we will discuss other ideas which will assist you in this endeavor.

The Value of the Social Mirror

We've been pretty hard on the social mirror in this chapter. There are many ways in which the social mirror can be one of our best tools in accomplishing the intent of the next part of our Personal Creed Document. Let's look at a few of them:

Letters from a friend or friends.

> You might want to identify one, two, three, or even four people with whom you have a relationship of trust, and have them participate with you in this exercise. When you ask them to participate, you will want to give them some structure to work within. Write them a letter which states something like the following:

Dear Friend,

I am involved in a project to understand myself better by getting feedback from special people with whom I have a relationship of trust. You are one of those people. I appreciate our friendship and feel comfortable that you can assist me in this endeavor so that I can see myself and what I communicate to others, by looking at myself through the eyes of another person. I will appreciate your perspective by answering the following questions:

a) When you think of me, what is the single most positive character trait that comes to your mind? Explain.

b) If you were commissioned to write a book (novel) with the objective to help others find meaning to their life by using me as a character; what role would you cast me in? What message would my life bring to the reader? Which of my character traits would you accentuate?

c) If you were asked to write an epitaph for the headstone to be placed on my grave, what would you write for generations to come to remember about my life?

d) What is one area you feel I could improve, as I seek to become a better person?

e) Do you have any advice for me as I continue to seek a happy, joyful personal and professional life? In other words, is there an area where you feel I ought to focus some effort to improve?

I appreciate your immediate response. Thank you for assisting me in my personal development project. I value your perspective.

Sincerely,

Many years ago near the conclusion of my final year in high school, one of my teachers conducted a most impressive exercise. The class size was moderately small, about twenty people. The teacher asked us to write a short paragraph to each of our fellow students, stating one positive attribute or characteristic that stood out in our mind, telling why we were grateful for that person. After we completed that exercise, we were invited to write an additional short paragraph (which he suggested should be about one-half as long as the first) issuing any advice we felt might be useful to each of our peers. He assured us at the outset that our comments would be held confidential. On completion, he collected the papers. During the next few weeks he compiled the comments into a typewritten individual document for each of us, containing the comments of our peers and his own added paragraph highlighting what he felt was our strong suit.

I will never forget the final moments of the last day we met in class when Mr. ____ distributed an envelope to each of us containing this document. While I couldn't wait to open it, I deferred until I found a place where I could be alone. Solemnly, with a quickened heartbeat and shaking fingers, I opened the envelope. It is difficult to explain the positive feelings I had when I carefully read, and then reread, the comments from a sampling of my peers who validated my existence as a human being. Comments in twenty short paragraphs provided an image of who David A. Christensen was in the eyes of his peers. I felt a special sense of worth as I read the words of my teacher who further sanctioned my existence. I felt ten feet tall! I liked me and I was glad I was alive! After I completed reading the positive declarations, I was ready to read the suggestions for improvement these great critics had to offer. My appreciation for my peers was so strong, at that point, that I read with an open heart and ready mind to understand what they felt I could do to be "even better than I already was." I enthusiastically accepted their suggestions. There was no "bristling" or animosity, whatsoever, in the counsel given or in the heart of the receiver.

That day currently ranks in the top ten most rousing and inspiring days of my life. As you read the foregoing, you may be critically saying to yourself "Oh, how nice!" or "That's too elementary or juvenile," or even "The author sure must have had a low self-esteem to have sucked in all that hype." If you would be against doing such an exercise, I invite you to ask yourself "Why not?" Are you threatened? Do you lack the kind of relationships which you will feel comfortable in asking for assistance from another? Are you threatened by knowing they might feel uncomfortable? Maybe the answers to the above questions will suggest something about yourself that can use some attention.

In the past several years I have personally experienced the value of that long ago day. The pages are now yellow, the typing a bit faded, and the edges tattered from being reviewed many times. The value of the social mirror can be incredible if set in a positive format. In addition to my own experience, I have witnessed feedback from many hundreds of students and seminar participants who report that similar exercises rank as one of their favorite personal development activities. When the social mirror validates our goodness, the experience is worthwhile!

Invite a handful of special people in your life to engage in an opportunity to share their view of who you are and what good things they see in your life and example. If you would prefer something more impersonal and a more professional approach, you may wish to use an electronically prepared profile that can be handed to several associates for their review and input. Then it can be compiled into a report for your study. The view and perspective of others can bring clarity and power to how you see yourself or where you choose to spend energy for improvement.

A Language to Honor Ourselves and Others

There are several excellent approaches to giving a positive understanding of ourselves and others. Some have created a language around animals, others with colors, and even others with seasons. In this book, I have chosen to utilize the language and systematic approach created by Dr. John Geier and Inscape Publishing. I appreciate their approach and recommend it to you for consideration. At the conclusion of this chapter I will provide further resource information for your review.

The Geier Approach looks at people with the view that each of us can be described and understood by our style of behavior. Behaviors are our distinct ways of thinking, feeling, and acting. There are four basic behavioral styles and nearly three hundred classical or combined styles. All have different ways of communicating, interacting, managing, leading, and living. Geier emphasizes that being "different" is all right.

Different is different, and it's not wrong. This is sometimes a difficult thing for people to renegotiate in their minds. We tend to have a structured attitude toward who is good and who is bad based on societal or cultural paradigm. I am not talking about the difference between good and evil or virtue and vice. I clearly subscribe to such standards. What I am talking about are the behavioral characteristics like confidence vs. cautiousness, imaginative vs. analytical, spontaneous vs. orderliness, decisive vs. investigative, and so on. Is it better to be confident or cautious? The answer is "yes!" It's better to be confident or cautious. Some would say, based on their own style of behavior or the paradigm they have formed from experience with leaders or loved ones, that decisiveness is the best. Others, by the same process have concluded that, it's best to think before you act—to decide only after appropriate analysis and investigation. Which is best? I suggest the answer is still "yes!" They are both best. The world needs the "decisive," just as it must have the "cautious." We need spontaneity just as we need orderliness. We need the behavioral diversity in people given us by the Creator. Can you imagine what the world would be like if everyone saw it in the same way? What if every human being was highly analytical? We would have a world in a perpetual state of trying to figure it out instead of living in it. We would become a giant laboratory analyzing analysis itself.

What would the world be like if everyone were "decisive" in the absence of "analyzers"? What a mess! Decisions would be made by every human being to a fault. We could predict a fair amount of conflict and chaos.

The key is in understanding that each style is good and important to the whole. We need the perspective and approaches of each style. We need each other. If we are normal, this concept will require a "Paradigm Shift" and for most, it will be a major shift in thinking. As a parent I have struggled with this. The extent to which I appreciate the different behavioral styles of my children, is the extent to which I not only enjoy them more, but meet their behavioral needs more completely and we all win. Life is better. Personal and family progress is stimulated and achieved. It is when I expect that my children should be behaviorally like me or see the world exactly as I do that we find conflict and we all lose. I think it is important to reemphasize that I am NOT talking about good vs. evil or virtue vs. vice. Nor am I talking about allowing ourselves, our children, and others to "do their own thing," or "to do whatever seems natural." I clearly believe in a Christian ethic and that there is good and bad, virtue and vice, and right and wrong. However, in the behavioral characteristic arena, I believe that the innate characteristics inherited from the Creator or the inborn stylistic tendencies are meant to be of benefit to the human family. I believe that there is no right or wrong behavioral style unless it is pushed to an extreme.

Let me explain. The Geier perspective teaches that the behavioral strengths of an individual pushed too far or overused can become their very weakness. Does that make sense? A person's strength, overused or overextended can, and usually does, become a personal weakness. In other words, back to the question "Is it best to be confident or cautious?" The answer is . . . "yes!" Both are best, good, desirable, and needed in the world. Each are strengths unless they are overextended or overused. If a person becomes too confident, that very strength or tendency becomes the Achilles Heel of the person. It becomes their weak or vulnerable spot in daily living. The over-confident will be overly decisive and make many wrong decisions. They will get themselves into jams, crises, and unwarranted messes because their estimation of their abilities exceed their capacity to perform. They often find themselves in predicaments and entanglements because they fail to prepare themselves to increase their competency and match their performance to the challenge. Their strength of confidence becomes their weakness, because it is out of balance and is overextended.

Likewise "cautiousness" is a positive virtue unless it is overused. There is something good about the person who will circumspectly and watchfully negotiate life. However, overextended, the strength quickly deteriorates into "STOP," "procrastination," or reverse momentum. The overcautious person will often be accused of stringing and unstringing their instrument, while the song they came to sing remains unsung. Cautiousness then becomes a debilitating weakness.

Each of the Behavioral Styles have different "needs" and "fears." A need is something a person seeks or moves toward, while a fear is something a person avoids or moves away from. Just as each of the four basic styles have different paradigms or maps of the way we see the world, each also have different needs and fears. The intent of each is to behave in such a way that their needs are met and their fears are avoided. In this sense, everyone is motivated! However they are motivated by THEIR needs and fears, and not the needs and fears of others. Take a minute and ponder this statement: "Everyone is motivated to do things for their reasons, not for your reasons." Their reasons are their needs and fears.

If each of us can understand ourselves better in terms of innate needs and fears, then we can approach living with a more calculated effort to meet those needs and avoid those fears. We can understand that "we aren't so bad after all"; that inborn characteristics are O.K. as long as we make an effort to keep them in check and not overextend them into weaknesses. The process of coming to know ourselves better has a wonderful spin-off benefit—we then understand others better and honor them for their differences. We become more tolerant of their "overextensions," because we see them for their strength instead of a bundle of weaknesses.

Using this language and understanding, we can honor and respect ourselves and others for our differences instead of gravitating to attitudes of "I wish you would be different" or "If only you were more like me." If we honor each other for our differences, we become more adaptable to others based on their needs and more sensitive to their fears. We avoid situations that will tread on those fears, because we appreciate their strengths. Our understanding compels us to like ourselves more, and to honor who we are and what we can become.

The Four Basic Styles

Geier's perspective identifies four basic styles. It is important to understand and constantly remember that we each possess all four styles. While we each have a measure of all four styles present, we tend to exhibit one or two styles more predominately in our behavior.

The styles are identified by the letters "D," "I," "S," and "C." "D" stands for Dominant or Directive. "I" stands for Interactive or Influencing. "S" stands for Steadiness or Supportive. "C" stands for Conscientious or Competent. Let's look at the basic characteristics of each style:

"D" style or "Dominant / Directive" individuals have a strong tendency toward high ego strength. They have a need to have their egos stroked and to be appreciated. They are naturally competitive and like to win. They are quick and like immediate results. They are goal oriented; setting and reaching goals is a form of giving feedback to their ego. They keep score. One of the significant characteristics of a high "D" behavioral style is that they need and enjoy change. They are the change agents of the world. They spend a lot of thinking time trying to figure out how to change things and make them better. They like direct answers to questions, preferring to cut through the verbiage and get to the bottom line. Their greatest fear motivator, something they avoid with passion, is being taken advantage of or not being in control of the situation. In fact, they will often take an offensive mode—doing things to gain control of a situation before it ever becomes a loss of control issue. One point worth making at this juncture is that most, if not all, anger and hostility arises out of situations where the behavioral "fear" is violated. In the case of the high "D," you can predict with extremely high probability, that the "D" is going to exhibit a behavior of anger if you arrest their control of any situation.

Let me illustrate. I have a high "D" son.- When the lawn needs to be mowed, I can take the approach of going to his room early in the morning and informing him that I want the lawn mowed by noon. In the high "D" mindset, that approach, suggests something like, "Hey, I am telling you to get out there and mow the lawn now." Does it leave any room for his need to control the situation? Not really! I have issued a command and expect that he is to respond by doing what I say. It sounds a little more like a puppet-puppeteer relationship. "D's" avoid loss of control or move toward gaining it. If Geier's thesis is true, that "D's" NEED control, what will my son do to get control back? He could exhibit a statement of anger by saying he has other things to do (things that he's in control of). He could choose to be in control of the "time" request and get me off his back by saying "OK," and then decide to do it tomorrow or later today or next week. He might even do it under my time demand of noon, but the job quality may fit his own guidelines, not mine. You see, one way or the other, he is going to be in control. If I make efforts to curb his control, he will strike back or exhibit some behavior to subtlety let everyone know ... "I'm in charge."

What would happen if I were to simply change my approach? If I remember "All people are motivated for their reasons and not mine" and "motivation comes from goals (something to move toward) and fears (something to avoid), then I can build my approach to the High "D" person accordingly. His needs come from an innate desire to be in "control." So I will build my request around that need, desire, or stylistic pattern. With this approach I would enter his room and say something like this: "Son, are you awake? Hey listen, what do you have planned today?" He might respond, "I'm really busy" or "I don't know yet, why?" I continue, "The lawn really needs to be mowed sometime today, or tomorrow at the latest. Do you think you can work it into your schedule?" I predict that if we have any kind of a relationship, he will respond and the lawn will get mowed in the time frame I gave him. It takes a little longer to make the request and in all reality, he may murmur or gripe that he's "over-worked and underpaid." But if I initiate my request with a mindset of meeting his need to be in control, he will usually respond. Why? Because I have identified the job, yet have given him freedom to decide which hour in the next thirty hours he will get it done. He is in control.

I can also consider other innate needs of the High "D," as I work on getting the lawn mowed. "D's" like ego stroking. They are competitive, quick, goal oriented, and like change. So I might infuse my request with a statement like, "I have never seen anyone get this little lawn job done faster or better than you, have you ever considered going into business? Maybe the neighbors would be interested in your services." As I meet his need to have his ego positively attended to, he responds. I might present my request with something like this: "Last week, you finished the lawn in about forty-five minutes. Five bucks say you can't do it with the same great quality you always do, in *less* than forty." In this approach I have attended to his "competitive nature," and I predict he will respond by completing it in thirty-eight minutes or less. Since "D's" like change and challenge, I might even try this approach: "We've been mowing the lawn every seven days through the summer months, can you think of another way to keep the lawn looking as nice with a different schedule?" Depending on the boy's age, you would be surprised at the solutions suggested. My twelve year old boy found out with one telephone call that we could treat our Arizona lawn with a growth retardant and reduce the mowing to once every three weeks. When he told me how much it would cost, I asked him to consider three other ways we could better spend the money to reduce his work load by sixty per cent and determine if it was worth it? He came up with the answers, not me. He was in control.

Do you get the idea? Each of us has "needs." When those needs are being met, we thrive and enjoy living, and when those needs are not met, we feel frustrated. If our "fears" are treaded upon, we tend to strike with anger or to carry unnecessary, retarding, resentment.

As you study the information in the following pages regarding individual styles, you will be able to extract some valuable understanding for your own immediate transition. Since our goal in transition is developmental, we can find in our study of behavioral style, how to better position ourselves to meet our needs. For example: If I were approaching the transition of going from high school to college, I would want be sure that my career choice was made with my innate "needs" in mind. I would create my educational plan, course work, relationships, class schedule, and completion goals around those needs. I would keep an eye on my strengths, and by understanding how my strengths overextended become my weaknesses, I could take deliberate action to avoid circumstances where those overextensions thrive. If I were in a midlife transition, a job change, or a divorce, I would look over past experiences and relationships to provide important answers to structure my next approach. In fact, usually midlife transitions and broken relationships find their roots in the negligence of "needs" or treading upon "fears." If you look closely at the job you have chosen to leave or the relationship fatality you've experienced, often you find that either your needs were not being met or perhaps "you" failed to see or consider the needs of others. Understanding ourselves provides not only a way to create an environment where we can thrive, but it also helps us to find ways to meet the needs of others so that they, too, blossom. Everybody wins! We can identify our strengths and therefore modify them before they extend into weaknesses. Further, we can identify the strengths, needs, and fears of a roommate, spouse, coworker, friend, or boss and by meeting those needs, we can positively accentuate their strengths. When we give others what they want and need, we usually get what we want and need.

The following pages give structured information regarding the four basic behavioral styles. As you study them, you will probably find that you will relate to all four styles in some way but will have one or two areas where you will find strong identification. We have all four styles in our behavior. However, we exhibit strong tendencies toward one or two. Understanding ourselves, allows us to predict behavior and ultimately plan for change, personal development, transformation, and realignment. If you have a desire to study your style more extensively, you may request information about a self-scoring personal profile system and other Inscape Publishing products by visiting my website at www.davidachristensen.com.

Behavioral Styles

Dominant or Directive

1. High Ego Strength. Need to have someone say "nice job," even though they innately feel accomplished in almost any endeavor.

2. Quick at what they do. Like to get things done. Very goal oriented. Movers and Shakers.

3. Desire Change. Like risk and new challenges. Courageous.

4. Need direct answers. Bottom-line thinking is their forte.

5. Fear loss of control or being taken advantage of.

Influencing or Interactive

1. Verbal. Emotional and expressive. They are not afraid to talk, meet new people, or promote themselves.

2. People oriented. They need people! It is not just that they like people, they need them around them. They are fun seekers anywhere people are found.

3. Spontaneous. React to life without concern for organization and forethought. For this reason, they are often disorganized.

4. Optimistic. Find opportunity in everything! They approach life from a Pollyanna paradigm; everything is possible and the universe is wonderful!

5. Fear loss of social approval. They love people and are very concerned about what others think of them. They want everything to be fun, happy, and positive. They are concerned that others are pleased with their contribution to the social circle.

Steadiness and Supportive

1. Very Loyal. They are some of the best friends anyone can ever have because they are excellent listeners. They accept others without prejudice and love to keep relationships very steady and happy.

2. Group or family oriented. Enjoy people for the memories and warm feelings they give.

3. Systematic, territorial, and possessive. Do things the same way, at the same time, and without a lot of variance.

4. Like sameness and need time to think about change.

5. Fear loss of security, change, and the unknown.

Conscientious, Compliant, and Competent

1. Are very orderly. Perfectionistic and have high personal standards.

2. Detail oriented. Precise. Need specific explanation. Need accuracy.

3. Extraordinarily intuitive. They seem to have a special sense for knowing causes and effects.

4. Private. It is often hard to build a relationship with these individuals as they seek to maintain and protect their perfect image.

5. Fear criticism of their work. Since they try very hard to do things well, their greatest fear is that their "best" won't be good enough.

ASSIGNMENT

It's time to consider Part Three of your Creed Document. This part focuses on you. If you have collected feedback from one or more people you trust in your social mirror, you may want to use their comments directly in this part of your Creed. As you have read the information on Behavioral Styles and identified your tendencies, you will likely want to include your findings in this process. The objective of this part of the Creed Document is to write one page, and no more than two, about yourself and your strengths. What makes you uniquely good? What do others who know you well, appreciate most about you? The Law of Uniqueness gives us permission to be wonderfully different than anyone else. What makes you wonderfully different? Given the notion that our strengths overextended or overused can expose personal weakness, write a paragraph about your awareness of your weakness and how that knowledge will assist you to improve.

I have hundreds of people every year tell me that this is one of the most energizing segments of their transitional quest to become better. Knowing who we are empowers us to grow. An awareness of the strengths, needs, and fears of others helps us in our efforts to lift them. When we lift others, we find the abundant life. Finding the abundant life through giving and building others, in turn, helps us find ourselves. Somehow, we become more substantive as we build others—indeed, it is easier to find ourselves because there is so much more of us to find! Understanding ourselves and others is an important key to positive transition.

Chapter Seven
LIVING BY VALUES

Let's take a look back over the first six chapters and review where we've been. Our objective is to seize transition as a time to move ourselves into a developmental, transformational, and realigning experience. We have acknowledged the value of "Time" in the quest for progress and have identified a method by which we can invest our time more wisely into activities which are most important in keeping first things first in our lives. We have discussed the concepts of Paradigms, Belief Windows, and their impact on our behavior. Further, we have identified a number of beliefs which we feel strongly about as fundamental paradigms for living. We have discussed the importance of "mentorship" in our lives and understand the incredible value of including others in shaping our view of the world. We have made an attempt to understand ourselves and others better to the end that we structure our transitional environment to meet "needs" and pay attention to "fears," which are the basis of all motivation. Additionally, in coming to understand the needs and fears of others, we can better serve them. Serving them helps us find ourselves and finding ourselves is a key to our development, transformation, and realignment quest.

You have been invited to engage in a process of building a blueprint for your life, which we call a Creed Document. We have identified several laws which govern causes and effects in our lives and accompanying Arts which are the learnable skills of applying our understanding of the Laws.

Now we are ready to begin what may be the keystone to this entire process. The identification and commitment to those things we value in our lives. Beliefs and values are very close cousins. Our beliefs are those opinions we have formed and accepted as real or true. They are based on real experience, vicarious experiences, or the opinions and perceptions of those we trust. Our values however are more attitudinal in nature and are the catalyst for ACTION. Our beliefs are perceptions of the way we see the world. Our values are what spur us to DO something about our perceptions. Often our values spring forth from our beliefs or are in some way an extension of our belief system, but they always spur us toward doing.

You may believe that democracy, a government for and by the people, is the best form of government based on your experience, study of history, or orientation provided by people you trust. However, whether or not you get out and vote on election day and participate as a citizen in the democratic process depends entirely on whether or not you really value the freedom democracy can bring.

You may believe that having good health is essential to living a full and happy life. Whether or not you get out and walk, swim, jog, or lose those extra twenty pounds depends on how much value you place on your own health.

You may believe in God or in the importance of right and ethical living. Whether or not you live in accordance with your understanding of right and wrong depends solely on the extent to which you value the benefits of doing so. Your beliefs about God or ethical living are perceptions only. The extent to which you are motivated to do something about those perceptions has to do with how much you value them.

Everyone has values. You probably feel that you have a fair sense of what your values are. Most people feel the same. Yet most people discover frustration in their lives because their ACTIONS are inconsistent with the principles or values they think they hold dear. Perhaps the reason for this inconsistency is because they really don't have a clear understanding of what they do value.

Transitional seasons are a natural time to examine values. In fact, it is a fairly simple process to look back at the outcomes of your past and identify certain actions which generated the results. Remember, ACTION is the result of what we Value, which is an extension of our Beliefs. As you examine your values and set a systematic approach to sharpen their capacity to direct your behavior, you will attain higher levels of success and happiness in your life.

Prior to launching into values identification and designing a system of living more congruently with them, let's consider a few more Laws, Arts, and Clues which will help us be more effective.

The Law of Entropy

Entropy finds its historical root in the Greek language having to do with "energy unavailable for useful work in effecting change in any system." Further definition of the word includes the synonyms disorder, disorganization, and uncertainty.

The Law of Entropy in a behavioral sense states: "Life unattended or neglected will naturally move toward a disorganized, undifferentiated state." In other words, the forces of entropy are constantly moving people toward a state of disorganization and mediocrity. Therefore, we can deduce that no human being will ever remain in a state of neutrality in terms of their progression or digression. Not paying attention to any dimension of life results in disorganization and digression. It can be seen in literally every arena of our lives. Let's look:

1. My desk unattended or neglected naturally moves toward an unorganized, undifferentiated state ... a mess. If I don't pay attention to keeping it tidy, it will get messy.

2. My body unattended or neglected will naturally move toward an unorganized, undifferentiated state. If I don't pay attention to it, exercise it, stretch its muscles, and feed it properly, its natural and normal definition will move toward being overweight, Baggy, stiff, and of ill health.

3. My family unattended or neglected will naturally move toward an unorganized, undifferentiated state. If I don't pay attention and make an effort to have a good family, nurture relationships, and make my home a haven from the challenges of a pretty vicious world, it will fail! If I don't take time to build and feed our relationship, my spouse and I will naturally grow apart until we just live in the same place and pass time tolerating one another instead of loving each other.

4. My mind, my job, my department, my business, my coursework, my scholastic standing, my 4H group, my yard, my finances, and literally everything ... unattended or neglected will naturally move toward a disorganized and undifferentiated state. Entropy simply says "PAY ATTENTION! OR COUNT ON EVENTUAL NEGATIVE RESULTS."

Perhaps we should be reminded that Laws don't care! The Law of Entropy has no feelings. It does not care whether you agree or not. It is simply a law, a function of the universe. If you are in college and don't go to class, study systematically, or talk to your academic advisor about your progress toward graduation, see what happens. If you are in sales and just sit around on the laurels of your past accomplishments, don't contact your customers for a year, put them on "hold" while you go fishing, watch what happens. If you are married and don't make any effort to spend time together to laugh, play, talk, think, and share—you know what will happen! Entropy is real! We must deal with this law!

Once I was teaching this concept to a group of employees from General Motors. A woman raised her hand and said, "To put it even more simply, what you are saying is `dead fish always float downstream.'" Simply stated, that's exactly it. If we don't pay attention and make an effort everyday to the things that matter most, we are in effect "dead fish" and entropy will automatically float us toward negative results. Another gentleman commented, "I don't know if I agree. Don't you think that sometimes things left alone get better?" I said "exactly." With real frustration he said "Now I know I don't understand or agree. You've been telling us that things left alone get worse and now you just admitted that things left alone can get better ... sometimes. What are you saying?" I responded "leaving things alone can be an ACTION where I have decided, after paying attention to an issue, that the best conduct is to do nothing. I am consciously choosing not give it my energy. That is different from just not paying attention." Does that make sense? When we make a choice not to exert our attention or efforts to something, to "put it on the back burner" for awhile, that decision is an action. There may be one exception in a thousand, where unintentionally leaving something alone makes it better. However, the general rule, the Law of Entropy demonstrates over and over again, "don't pay attention ... expect it to become worse."

The Art of Progressive Living

Since the forces of Entropy move us toward a disorganized and undifferentiated state, we must acquire the skill and learn the Art of Progressive Living. We must learn how to wake ourselves up and pay attention to the things in life which we value. Learning to be alert and mindful of what will happen to us behaviorally if we allow the powers of entropy to take over, is a virtue worth working toward. Let's identify a continuum model. The right side of the continuum is Digressive Living and the left side is Progressive Living. When we apply the Law of Entropy to this model, we note that when one does not pay attention to any dimension of their life, they will naturally move toward the right side of the model to "Digressive Living." In other words, by not expending energy to move toward "Progressive Living" they, like the "dead fish" definition given by my Detroit seminar participant, are always going to "float downstream" toward the disorganization and undifferentiation of "Digressive" behavior.

It takes constant effort to move to the left side of the model. It takes energy and labor to live progressively. The natural man and woman have a tendency to move to the right side of the model, unless they give constant and consistent toil to move toward progressive living. Does that make you tired just to think about it? Progressive Living is a way of life, not a destination. It's striving, working, and constantly endeavoring to become aware. When we slack off even for a day or week, the forces of Entropy gently nudge us backward, and we float toward the right side of the model. Simply put, we must be constantly and anxiously engaged in doing what it takes to be progressive.

Now, let's look at the model as a way to graphically understand what happens in everyday life. All day, everyday, we move back and forth across the model. We pay attention and we are able to move ourselves to the left, we let up and allow our attention to be diffused by unimportant distractions and we will float back to the right. We "wake up," figuratively speaking, and pay attention to the things that matter most and we move back to the left. This happens over and over again. It's part of the turf of earth life and it's O.K.! There is nothing wrong with the constant challenge to keep moving toward more progressive living and there is nothing inherently wrong with falling backward so long as we don't give up in defeat and concede to living digressively as a way of life. That's the great tragedy of life—when a person with limitless capacity gives up, decides that striving is too hard, throws in the towel, and gives himself or herself permission to live permanently and effortlessly on the right side of the model. 'What a tragedy! The truth is, most human beings don't consciously choose defeat. It is not in our nature. However, masses of the human family are lulled away into unconscious defeat. Most aren't even aware of where they are in the model—they don't know they've trapped themselves in digressive, "go-nowhere," "be nobody" lifestyle. The tragedy is in living day to day in quiet and effortless desperation and not even realizing it.

The Art of Progressive Living is the skill of paying attention, then exerting the effort to move ourselves out of digressive behavior. If we pay enough attention and move ourselves to the left enough times, we will find that the

Behavior Continuum

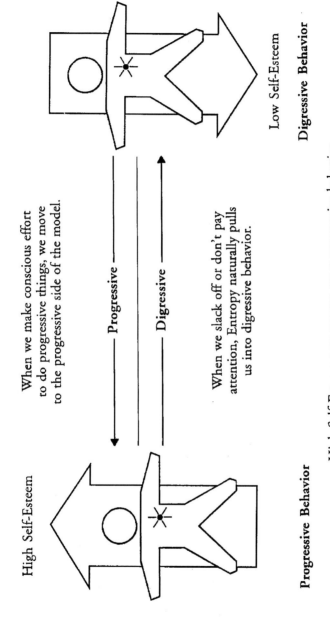

When we make conscious effort to do progressive things, we move to the progressive side of the model.

High Self-Esteem

Progressive

Digressive

When we slack off or don't pay attention, Entropy naturally pulls us into digressive behavior.

Low Self-Esteem

Progressive Behavior

Digressive Behavior

High Self-Esteem perpetuates more progressive behavior.
Low Self-Esteem tends to produce more digressive behavior.

inertia decreases at the same as time our capacity to move increases, and we develop a habit of living progressively. I appreciate the statement of Aristotle "Excellence is an art won by training and habitation. We do not act rightly because we have the virtue of excellence but rather we have those because we have acted rightly. We are what we repeatedly do. Excellence, then is not an act but a habit." However, though living progressively becomes easier when its habitual, if we let up or slack off, Entropy moves us back to the right. The Art of Progressive Living then, is being aware of where we are on the continuum and doing what it takes to move ourselves where we want to be, over and over again until it becomes a habit.

Digressive Living

Let's develop an understanding of the behavioral tendencies of the right side of the model. Knowing the characteristics of digressiveness leavens our alertness to catch ourselves and give conscious effort to move to a more progressive type of behavior.

1. **Worry.** A hallmark of digressive behavior is "worry." When we worry, we are constantly concerned with what "might happen if." We stew and stress, depleting our energy to act. We become disabled and handicapped by our fears. Our most dominant thoughts are more about what might go wrong instead of what we can do to solve the problem.

Now remember, why are we identifying these characteristics? We are identifying them so that we catch ourselves and move ourselves back toward the progressive behavior side of the model. For example, if I were to catch myself worrying I would say to myself, "David, this is stupid! It isn't productive. In fact, it *is* weakening to my ability to think and act. Now get back over to the other side and do something about this problem if you can, and if you can't, forget about it! Engage yourself in something that will make a positive difference."

2. **Excusitis.** Digressive behavior is punctuated by excuses. You can even hear this one in the idle chatter of those who are going nowhere. "I couldn't because ... ," "If only I would have ... ," "I was late because ... ," "It was his fault," and "I didn't know ..." Digressive behavior exhibits excuses for everything that does not go right or as desired.

3. **Finger Pointers.** Blame is a twin of excusitis. It is an attempt to shift responsibility away from *self* to someone else when life doesn't go the way we think it should. "I would have gotten a better grade in calculus, but the teacher was boring." Do you see the shift of responsibility in that excuse? "I'm smart but boring teachers are responsible for my lack of performance." Or how about this one, "I would have gotten the promotion, but my associate had more political advantage." Another might be, "We could have had a better marriage, if you hadn't have been so selfish." Digressive behavior *is* found in blaming and not accepting an appropriate share of the problem. Ironically, when we shift the blame to others, we in reality, give up control of living our own lives by admitting we are puppets controlled by the strings of others.

4. **Perception of Failure.** When we are in a digressive mind set, we tend to see failure as terminal. We see it as an extension of who we are and automatically assign the result to our character. We even expect it to happen. Have you ever said or heard someone else say, "I knew that it wouldn't work!" or "I told you so." It *is* almost like they are waiting for failure to happen, since they expect it. When failure does occur, it *is* always someone else's fault.

5. **Low Self-Esteem.** Digressive behavior is wrought with Low Self-Esteem. When we don't like ourselves or depreciate our capacities to be progressive, we do more dumb things. These actions feed and give life to lower self-esteem, which in turn perpetuates doing more dumb things, and it becomes a vicious cycle. Worry, excusitis, blaming, failure, and all digressive behavior is laced with Low Self-Esteem.

6. **Externally Focused.** Since the self-esteem of a person engaged in digressive behavior is extraordinarily low, they attempt an external focus to decrease the pain. They are obsessed with how they look, the kinds of clothes they wear, the cars they drive, labels, status, and quantity. They attempt to get self-worth by having things. They rely on the reactions of others to their apparent success to nurture and give balm to their wounded self-esteem. It works pretty well until they lose their toys, their clothes wear out, their hair falls out, and their wrinkles set in. When you strip away the external and they are left naked, without possessions, their true self-worth emerges again

in frustration. We can sometimes identify this low self-esteem in the way we talk, what we talk about, and how we say it. Digressive behavior, in this regard, will do anything to bring attention to the wounded *self.* Sometimes we will be loud, talk excessively about why we're special, or invite others to comment on our meritorious life. External trappings, external commentary, and what others can see is at the heart of digressive low self worth.

7. **Indecisiveness.** There is a difference in being analytically indecisive and being incapable of making a decision due to preoccupation with what other people will think. Since self-esteem is so low in people who live digressively, they are overly concerned about how their main source of individual validation (their peers) will react. It is difficult to decide what to wear, whether to accept a date with a person outside the norms dictated by their social circle, what color of car to drive, or how they must dress for success.

8. **"If I had, then I could" Syndrome.** A syndrome is defined as a set of characteristics which identify a certain condition or disease. This condition is a disease for sure. It is characterized by a constant attitude that happiness, enjoyment, and success are found in some thing or some condition which one does not yet have. Here are several examples: "If I just had a new computer, then I could get my work done faster," "If I just had ten thousand dollars and my debts all paid off, then I would really be happy," "If I had a different professor, then I would be more interested in the subject matter," "If I had that job on the twentieth floor of the Prudential Building, then I could really enjoy life," "If I just had a different spouse, a newer car, a better job, more toys, less weight, nicer clothes, THEN I would be really happy." Success, happiness, and enjoyment are always conditional upon the possession of a certain something or an environment that is different from what we do have. I appreciate something my parents often quoted, "So many people in the world are looking for the way to happiness, when all the time HAPPINESS is the way." Digressive Behavior is manifest by an incessant illusion that the key to the happiness and success is found in a possession or condition somewhere out there. When the person with this syndrome achieves the condition or acquires the possession (when they get that computer, that new spouse, or the new automobile), guess what? In time (usually, a short time), if you listen

closely you will hear familiar echoes. There will be something else they lack, some condition not currently available upon which their happiness rides. The syndrome is characterized by the individual spontaneously fabricating another something, someone, or condition which will bring success, happiness, and enjoyment. "If I had, then I could" is a real syndrome worth paying attention to, especially in transitional periods of life. Many people have discovered that their transitions in life revolve almost solely around this syndrome. Recognition of this "disease" enables us to move ourselves to the left side of the continuum. Some people find that they really have had all the ingredients for success and happiness, but were blinded by the constant yearning pains of the "If I had, then I could" Syndrome. Do a self examination and diagnosis for this condition. All of us seem to get it sometime. Left unchecked and uncontrolled, it can be the undoing of an otherwise successful and happy life.

9. **Reactive.** Digressive behavior is almost always reactive. Responding only when stimulated usually brings frustration. If the only time we act is when we are acted upon, we have a Puppet and Puppeteer relationship with life. The puppet only moves when the puppeteer pulls the strings. When on the right side of our Progressive-Digressive Continuum, reactive people respond to life only when the stimulus is strong enough. In other words a reactive student begins intensive study only when the stimulus of a major test is coming tomorrow.... now it's cram time! A reactive employee springs into productive action only when the heat is turned up and the crisis of needing work completed yesterday is on! A reactive parent waits until their child is in trouble before they spend time with them. Reactive people have a stimulus addiction. Their actions are dependent upon the degree and intensity of the stimulus. Mild stimulus gets mild response. Heavy stimulus gets immediate strong response. Since stimulus dictates action, reactive mentality requires a search for reasons to absolve responsibility. It's then that those engaged in this digressive mode resort to excusitis, the blame game, and a feeling of helplessness.

10. **Fear Motivated.** Why do you do what you do? Does it have more to do with fear, duty, or love? When the main source of motivation to act is rooted in "fear," we can know that it is the food for digressive behavior. Why do you work? Why do you attend college? Why

do you marry? If the answers to these questions are because "If I don't work they will kick us out of the house, we will starve, and I will be unemployed," or "If I don't go to college I am afraid I won't get a good paying job," or "If I don't stay married then I'll be alone and nobody else will want me"; then fear motivates actions. If our answers come from "I am supposed to," then duty stimulates the response. We will discuss later the details of "love motivation," but if my answer comes from "I love my work," "I love learning and preparing for my future," and "I love her/him and care deeply for their happiness," then our action is motivated by the greatest of all motivations—Love.

11. **Hold Grudges.** With the self-esteem factor at its lowest on the digressive side of the continuum, holding a person in emotional debt against some past deed seems to artificially inflate one's self worth. If we can mentally keep others indebted to us with a grudge, we erroneously feel that somehow makes us superior. Interestingly, studies universally verify that people tend to harbor grudges against their parents as being the culprits for our defeats and shortcomings. Only God gets more blame than parents, followed by a long list of people who have somehow crossed sensitive lines, fed professional jealousies, and otherwise treated us unkindly. We will dedicate part of a chapter to this issue later in the book. But suffice us to say at this point, a major characteristic of digressive behavior is blaming and shifting responsibility for life's inconveniences to a "grudge list" of "unforgivables."

12. **"I" Trouble.** How everything affects "me" is central to digressive thought. "I" am the center of the universe and all revolves around me. This is another low self-esteem manifestation worth identifying in ourselves from time to time. There are others in this world with different needs. There are a whole host of variables that do make a difference in what I should do, how I should act, and most importantly, who I am and what I can do to make this world better. Digressive attitudes and action are out of focus and blur reality through "I" trouble.

Progressive Living

Let's move across the model and identify those behavioral clues of being

---

progressive. When we do find ourselves on the right side of the model, we can consciously move ourselves to the left side and substitute digressive behavior with progressive behavior. If we catch ourselves enough times and move ourselves toward more progressive behavior, in time we will spend more time on the left side and progressive living will become habitual. We will enjoy life more and be more successful. Here are a few of the hallmark behavioral characteristics of progressive people:

1. **Happy**. I find it extremely interesting that in *Webster's New World Thesaurus,* the first antonym given for "worry" is "happy." Perhaps that is because when we liberate ourselves, from worry, we have the power to be happy. Progressive people do encounter worrisome issues in their lives just like anyone else. The difference is that they understand that worry is an activity that will not bring any worthwhile results. Hence, they choose to engage in activity or thought processes that are problem solving or completely abandon conscious thought about the issue. When they stop worrying, they tend to move to happier thought. They simply refuse to spend time and energy on thoughts and internal churning where nothing can be done to control the outcomes. If they determine that some action can control or effect outcomes, they spend their energy DOING and not thinking about it.

2. **"I am Responsible!"** Perhaps the cornerstone of progressive living is bedded on the foundation of "personal responsibility." Remember digressive characteristics of excusitis, finger pointing, and playing the proverbial blame game. "I am responsible" is one of the most important phrases etched forever in the mind of the happy person. The instant we take responsibility for how we react to life's experiences and avoid crediting discomfort or even success, to fortune, destiny, or the next person, is the day we find the freedom to be happy. We will refer again to Dr. Viktor Frankl's best selling book entitled, *Man's Search For Meaning*—perhaps a brief reference to his insights would be appropriate at this juncture. In the Nazi death camps of Germany, Dr. Frankl learned that man does have the responsibility and choice of action. Everything can be taken from you except one thing—the power to choose your attitude in any given set of circumstances, to choose your own way. We have the freedom and responsibility to choose how we react to life.

Instead of blaming a boring teacher for our substandard grade in History Class, be responsible for how we react to his lectures and choose to find a road to reading and comprehending on our own. WE ARE RESPONSIBLE! When we search for excuses or reasons why we are unhappy or not as lucky as someone else—WE ARE RESPONSIBLE for how we react to life, not someone else, the weather, or luck.

3. **Failure is Fertilizer.** While digressive mentality grovels in failure as a terminating, life-ending, saga of life; progressive individuals find the instructional components of it. Failure is a part of the process of success, not a terminal outcome. One of the best known and often used examples of progressive thought is from the *Memoirs of Thomas Edison*. The story tells how Thomas had been making what seemed an endless series of experiments in his quest to invent the incandescent light bulb. Once a reporter questioned Mr. Edison about his inability to produce a product that would bring what was then referred to as "artificial light" to man. "Mr. Edison" he said, "when will you concede that this quest is not possible, your assistants report that you have tried and failed over 5,000 times to find a process that will give mankind artificial light. Your peers in the scientific world postulate that your effort is commendable but impossible. After so many failures (5,000) when will you concede that it cannot be done?" Thomas replied, "We have not failed 5,000 times! We have succeeded in identifying 5,000 combinations that will not work, isn't that exciting?" Thomas Edison knew that failure was an integral component of success. He produced the light bulb enjoyed by mankind, but he had to first fail in excess of 5,000 times in order to succeed. Similar stories are told of his attempts to develop the battery and other inventions we find commonplace today.

If you listen closely, you can hear progressive talk all around you. "I am not glad we had that financial failure, but we learned so much." "I regret that our relationship didn't work out, but I do know I learned a great deal from our experience." "I didn't get the grade I wanted in that class, but I did learn something about my study habits that may make a big difference in the balance of my formal educational experience." Success is in learning from failure. Failure is the fertilizer that produces success.

4. **High Self-Esteem.** Progressive people like themselves. They have the capacity to enjoy living because they are pleased with who they are. They accept improvement as a part of life and are aware of their deficiencies. They find that when they feel good about themselves, their output is better, and when their output is better they feel even better about who they are. They also recognize that when they do not produce, they sense a lower self-esteem and that creates substandard output, which in turn promotes even lower self-esteem. Self-Esteem is effected by output and Entropy demands a conscious effort to move ourselves toward the left side of the model. Recognizing this motivates them to do something to reverse self-defeating behavior by scoring a victory or two, even if they are small.

5. **Internal Focus.** While digressive behavior is manifested by external focus, progressive behavior is distinctly exhibited by an absolute internal attitude. It's not what we own, what we drive, how well we dress, or how many trappings and toys we've accumulated that evidences how successful we are. The low self-esteem of "digressives" motivates them to move to external evidences, but "progressives" are different. They have a quiet love affair with themselves (I like to use the acronym QLA). When we are progressive, although we may have our share of external trappings, we don't depend on them for our self-worth. We operate not "from what I have" but rather "from who I am." There is a quiet peace in knowing who we are. That, my friends, is what this whole book and exercise is about. We will find ourselves as we define what we believe, how we are uniquely good, and create relationships with others which compliment who we are. Progressive behavior and attitude *is* rooted deeply in "who I am."

6. **Decisive.** While there is nothing wrong with being deliberate decision-makers, we may need to take a look at why we have a hard time making decisions. If we are driven by "what others think" verses "what is right or best" as we engage in the decision process, then maybe we have discovered a clue of digressive behavior. The application of the Law of Entropy will then motivate us to move to the left side of our imaginary continuum and make decisions more quickly on the basis of moral, spiritual, or ethical perspective. Progressive people have a deep-seated set of moral or ethical values to operate from—therefore, choosing the right alternative or making the right decision is easier and done more quickly.

7. **Proactive.** While living reactively means that our daily living is filled with reactions to external stimulus, proactive living comes from an entirely different mind-set. Proactivity means we live life because of our capacity to choose our response. Conscious choice is the basis of the proactive life. Our behavior *is* a function of our decisions and the choices we make, not our environment or conditions. The power to choose and the freedom to find our way is the basis of a proactive life. Dr. Stephen Covey in his excellent book, *The Seven Habits of Highly Effective People,* states, "The ability to subordinate an impulse to a value is the essence of the proactive person.... their response to the stimuli, conscious or unconscious, is a value-based choice or response.... It's our response to what happens to us that hurts us." Proactive people understand that we are responsible for the way we react, or put another way we are able to choose our response to any stimuli. Proactive people are always acting upon what "can be done." They choose not to grovel in "what if s" and "I cannot's." They make choices to "proact" or do what they choose instead of being a puppet reacting to all of the things that are going wrong because somebody else didn't do something right. They respond to the "I will do with what I have, in the best way I can" mind-set.

8. **Love motivated.** The inner drive for progressive people is Love. "I love life with all of its challenges, hard times, good times, and surprises" is the way progressive people operate. They do what they do because they LOVE. They love life, so they live it! They enjoy their work because they love what they are doing. They love those they associate with because of their individual uniqueness. Their sense of service comes from a heart that LOVES others. They LOVE their environment whether its cold, hot, dry, wet, or windy. They choose to enjoy it all! LOVE for life, experience, challenge, and others is the root of what makes them tick. Progressive people are motivated by love—not fear or duty, but LOVE.

9. **Forgiving.** This attribute of progressive living is so important, we will dedicate a whole chapter to it later in this book. However, it is worth mentioning that one of the special characteristics of progressive people is their capacity to see how silly it is to live life holding senseless grudges. They forgive and forget! In a real world sense they may struggle a bit with the insensitive actions of others, but they are quick to recognize that the energy being expended on some past

deed of another person, a past circumstance, or an unfortunate happening is useless at best. They work through their issue quickly and simply bury it deep within the past. They choose to direct their energy toward living today and not in the mistakes and circumstances of the past. It is easy to see how much more energy and focus they have, simply because it is not tied up or directed in the "grudge."

10. **"We" focused.** While digressive people live their lives in "I" trouble, progressive people see life as an interdependent exercise where people live together, work together, strive together, and help each other. "We are working on this issue," "we have a problem," "what can we do?" and "we are finding a solution" are the talk of the progressive. Interdependent thinking is how progressive people see life. What we choose to do, does effect others. What we do to enhance each others lives will ultimately make us all better.

Summary

The Law of Entropy is real! I have been teaching the Law of Entropy (from a behavioral perspective) for the past several years. When I meet former students or receive letters from them, they relate their appreciation in understanding this law. They remember a continuum, which on the right side is marked "digressive" and the left side "progressive." They see that we are either making effort to move to the left, or without an expenditure of constant effort, we are naturally drifting or floating to the right side. As we move to the left our self-esteem is appropriately inflated, as we move to the right our self-worth lessens. Our capacity to live and enjoy life is increased on the left while we sense frustration and inner defeat on the right. My former students tell me it is one of the most powerful reminders and has made a difference in their daily living. They understand that all dimensions of their life "unattended or neglected" naturally move to an unorganized, undifferentiated state." They know they must always keep trying and striving, which naturally accelerates their "becoming." The Law of Entropy is real.

Chapter Eight

EXPECTATION

Have you ever thought much about expectation theory? Why do some people seem to have all the luck and others inevitably go from one fall to the next? Is it destiny, foreordination, fate, or karma? For some, life seems to produce a certain amount of difficult and unexplainable circumstances, while others seem to glide almost effortlessly from one success to another. Perhaps there is a certain amount of fortune or predetermination to the outcomes of our lives. However, I believe that if we look closely, we will discover that most of the results in our lives come from what we expect. I can't help but believe, as I examine the lives and outcomes of my greatest heroes, that they had an element of• faith, trust, and expectation that they would succeed or realize positive outcomes in their lives. I've also noticed that many of those who fall into the mud of life or have constant scrapes with misfortune have an expectation that they will fall or that they are not worthy of successful outcomes. It even appears that some people get onto a successful track and then mysteriously spiral into a fateful crash. Careful examination will often show these people have what Dennis Waitley calls "permanent potential." They almost succeed and then fail. It is almost as if some inner message is sent, saying "Who do you think you are? You aren't worthy of the success you are about to achieve! Don't you know that the kind of victory you are about to score is for people who are more credible, meritorious, or more deserving than you? Come now, get back down!" These "almost winners" then slow down or exhibit some self-defeating behavior that insures their defeat.

This book is about the "inner" or "private" victory in our lives. Expectation is private. Expectation is inner. Expectation is attitudinal. It also springs forth from the well of such character traits as faith, trust, confidence, certitude, and self-assurance through understanding that we can all be worthy of total success, happiness, and enjoyment.

It seems that in the transitional seasons of our lives, we need to examine, even more, the implications of this important principle or law. When we desire positive change, development, transformation, and realignment in our lives, it is important to check our "expectation quotient." How have our past expectations impacted the outcomes in our life? How can we sharpen our current expectations into driving forces for realization of the transformation and realignment we hope to find in the future?

The Law of Expectation

The Law of Expectation states: "That which we expect with a high degree of confidence will likely become a reality." I remember as a little boy listening to my mother tell me the story of the little engine who "thought" it could. The story was first published in 1930 and has been cherished by many readers and listeners for nearly seventy years. It is an inspiring children's story about a little blue train engine who overcame the obstacles of many older, wiser, and more experienced train engines, who thought a task of getting over a huge mountain was impossible (especially for a *little* engine). In the most difficult trials of its effort to beat the odds, the little engine draws upon its internal dialogue by thinking "I think I can, I think I can, I think I can, . . . " Her capacity to perform was increased and with great effort and focus upon the purpose to deliver toys to the children on the other side of the mountain, she climbed and conquered the crest of the mountain and chugged down the opposite side saying, "I thought I could, I thought I could, I thought I could, . . . "

It was one of my favorite stories. "belief" is one of the most powerful basic first principles of living. "Trusting or having faith" that life is going to turn out all right, or even great, is a foundational law worth paying attention to. Expecting the attainability of reaching the crest of the mountain, and anticipating the spiritual and emotional exhilaration of arrival and enjoyment, is fundamental to making it. That which we expect with a high degree of confidence will likely become reality.

Unfortunately, it goes both ways. Expecting defeat, or expecting to get halfway up the mountain then deciding it isn't worth it, is just as real. The little engine "thought it could" and never considered that it could not. Considering, thinking, and dwelling on what can never happen, will produce the kinds of inner defeat that insure public defeat or mediocrity.

I love my parents! They are among the most adored people in my life. They are human and so are you and I. I loved hearing the story of *The Little Engine that Could* and I am sure the moral of its message has been a blessing to my life. In addition to internalizing the message of this inspiring story, I was also internalizing other conflicting messages given by my environment. They were messages like: "you are shy and quiet," or "work is much more important than play ... people who waste their time playing all the time are worthless," or "you can't afford expensive things ..." In other words, "being quiet is a real liability in this life, work is the essence of living, and dreaming of a good and happy life is not appropriate." You may be saying "Come on, David! How in the world could you get those kinds of interpretations or messages from loving people who were simply trying to teach you important things about life? Give them a break—they were doing their best!" I do give them a break. In fact, I completely agree that parents, teachers, and leaders are usually well-intended. We all intend to do the very best we can for those we love the most. I too, struggle with the gap between my intentions and my communications. You see, communication *is* so delicate. What I say and how it is interpreted is the challenge! While I know others intended to be helpful, I cannot apologize for my interpretation of the messages they send! Whether it was wrong or stupid or totally inappropriate, it is how I understood it.

I am grateful to my mother for instilling the "I Think I Can" paradigm which gave me the power to work through all of the other paradigms which haven't served me well. It has been difficult to overcome the negative expectations I interpreted from loving parents, well intentioned teachers, and coaches who may have forgotten the losing impact they were having on their players while they thought they were winning because of the numbers on the scoreboard.

I believe that if you will look closely at your life, you will find some equally inaccurate interpretations that have found their way into your "expectations." We all live with certain expectations which most often turn into realities. Can you identify those which have no positive place in your life? Will you check them to see which ones need to be remodeled and which ones you will want to sharpen and use even more in your daily life? Anthony Robbins says "Nothing has any power over me other than that which I give it through my conscious thoughts." Our power to move into positive transitions *is* dictated to a large degree by what we are willing to give our conscious thoughts to. Are we anticipating the best and most desirable results? Are we prepared to eliminate the negative expectations that sabotage our success? Paul J. Meyer, a student and teacher of success models, once stated "Whatever you vividly imagine, ardently desire, sincerely believe, and enthusiastically act upon ... must inevitably come to pass." *The Little Engine that Could* did so because it thought it could. "Thinking you can" has less to do with Positive Mental Attitude than it does with character driven traits like Faith, Trust, and Confidence. Cultivating character traits brings lasting and more accurate expectations than do personality ethics. Seeing the world through the eyes of confidence in positive outcomes *is* the essence of the Law of Expectation.

The Art of Positive Self-Talk

Did you know that, depending on your age, you have several trillion messages recorded on the "personal computer" of your brain? Almost inconceivable to consider, isn't it?

Trillions of messages accepted and stored. The internal sort function of our brain is categorizing, filing, and making sense of all of this information. Some of it is filed in the "unimportant data" file, while chunks of it are processed and stored for frequent retrieval. Some behavioral scientists suggest that we have about 100,000 bits of data that we use repeatedly.

This data base of messages and information serves as a core of internal dialogue which we have with ourselves. This internal dialogue is called "Self-talk." We are constantly engaged in self-talk. For twenty-three hours each day we talk to ourselves either consciously or subconsciously, even when we are asleep. Most scientists agree that during the deepest portion of our sleep pattern (about one hour), self-talk is not taking place. Do you know what that means for you? For every year of your life since about age four, you having been talking to yourself for 8,400 hours or in excess of a half million minutes per year. For me, that means I've been cycling and recycling the data I have allowed to dominate my internal dialogue for over twenty million minutes or 335,800 hours. If I've allowed my data script to include erroneous assumptions or information which fosters negative feelings about who I am or what I can or cannot do, can you see the impact it can have on the outcomes of my life? What about your internal dialogue and self-talk script? If you're normal, you likely have never paid much attention to the way you talk to yourself.

If you listen closely you will find that most of your internal conversation centers around some form of two statements. We are almost constantly cycling and recycling a form of these two powerful scripts: "It's like me" or "It's not like me." Over and over again we confirm and reconfirm who we are and who we are not, what we can do and what we cannot, and thus create a long list of our ability or lack of capacity to measure up in certain areas of our lives. Leading behavioral research informs us that nearly seventy-seven percent of everything we think is in a negative form. In other words, we've accepted the wrong kind of programming. We each accepted a lot of data,

---

word after word, year after year, layer by layer, as programming for what has become our self-esteem. We began to believe the negative input of others and at some point made a decision to accept it as "truth." In his excellent book *What to Say When You Talk to Yourself* Shad Helmstetter gives us a perspective worth considering. "In the last two decades we have learned more about the workings of the human brain than was known throughout all history prior to that time. We now know that by an incredibly complex physiological mechanism, a joint effort of body, brain, and mind, we become the living result of our own thoughts.... how successful you will be at anything is inexorably tied to the words and beliefs about yourself that you have stored in your subconscious mind. You will become what you think about most; your success or failure in anything, large or small, will depend on your programming—what you accept from others, and what you say when you talk to yourself. The brain simply believes what you tell it most. And what you tell it about you, it will create. It has no choice."

I have come to believe with all my heart that Self-Talk may be one of the most important functions to determine outcomes than anything else. In fact, I invite you to consider the following statement as one you'll embrace:

> Everything in my life begins, continues,
> and ends with the way I talk to myself.

I know the word "Everything" is a big, all inclusive word. However, we know that the subconscious mind cannot differentiate the real from the unreal. If our internal dialogue is on "play" twenty-three hours per day, 8,400 hours per year, and over a half-million minutes every twelve months, then I choose to acknowledge that my self-talk or internal dialogue is going to effect how I act and what kind of outcomes I experience. Whether or not it is "everything" or "most" or "many," I believe serious attention should be given to this major influence on our behavior.

Let's look closer. Some years ago we lived in a suburb community of Phoenix. We had acquired a home in a nice neighborhood of acre lots. The developer had zoned the property so that each homeowner had animal rights, or the opportunity to have horses or cattle. We chose to raise a couple of calves. The home in back of ours had been vacant for some time, but on the day I brought my new calves home and released them into the pasture, I noticed a moving van unloading at the home. We were delighted to have new neighbors. An hour later, I observed a horse trailer pull up to the pasture adjoining ours and release an Arabian horse which began to run the perimeter of our common fence line. It was beautiful!

As the evening approached, it began to rain. My son came running into the house and informed me that our calves had discovered a way to escape through the back fence. I proceeded to recorral them and reinforce the fence line they would be contained. I was working fast as a drizzling rain hampered my progress to complete the containment before it got dark. As I was working on the fence, I glanced through the downpour toward the newcomer's home and saw my new neighbor for the first time. He had on a western hat and, as near as I could tell, he was wearing a denim jacket. The most visible characteristic of this new resident was that he was wheeling his wheelchair through the wet muddy pasture toward me. I confess, that moment, I did not want to take the time to meet him, entertain him, or spend my valuable last few minutes of "daylight," talking and exchanging neighborly pleasantries. I pretended not to have seen him and directed my attention toward my task. Almost before I knew it, I heard his voice. "Good evening," he said, "Can I help you? I'm your new neighbor!" Again, I confess, I thought, "I'm busy, can't he see there might be a better time for meeting?" Then before I knew it, he had launched himself from his wheelchair to the ground, and was at my side with a set of pliers in his hands ready to assist me. "Hello, I'm Dave," he said, holding out his gloved hand. I responded "Pleased to meet you Dave, my name is also Dave." It was nearly dark and while I could not see any details, I did note that his face was about fifty percent covered with burn scars. He had no legs; they had been amputated several inches above the knees. Immediately he sat on the ground next to the fence I was mending and assisted until the job was done. That was my first meeting with our new neighbor. In the days and weeks that followed, I came to love and respect this great man. He was a National Champion in cutting horse competitions, he snow skied, played catch (baseball) with his two sons, and ended up coaching a men's basketball team in a community league which I played on. He inspired us to championship status. One of the most impressive visits we had was when he privately told me of the event which took his legs and scarred his face. He, like thousands of others our age, spent time in Vietnam. He was driving a jeep ahead of his platoon when it hit a land mine. It blew up his jeep, injuring him significantly and rendered him unconscious for weeks. Sometime later in a hospital, he regained consciousness and found himself lying in a sterile hospital bed. His entire body was wrapped in gauze bandages except for one of his eyes and part of his nose. He laid there on the bed for a few moments trying to think of who he was, where he was, what happened, etc. Then he made an effort to sit up in bed. When he did so, he recognized something was different. The counter weight of his legs was gone, and he noticed two little bumps rise up in the sheets in front of him. It was then that he realized his legs were amputated. While the realization was a shock, he told me that the most difficult time came in the minutes, days, and even years after when we would be lying on the bed and feel an itch in his toes, or a pain in his ankle, or a twitch in his calf muscle. While his conscious mind knew and understood he had no legs, ankles, or toes, he could feel sensations in each. His subconscious mind had been programmed for nearly twenty years that he had fully functioning limbs. When they were removed, that didn't change his subconscious programming.

Our subconscious mind, programmed by the constant internal self-talk, has a powerful impact upon what we feel, sense, and ultimately do. My friend told me that, even years later, he would feel tingling in his lower legs or would get up in the night to go check on one of his children and would find himself on the floor beside his bed, having fallen as he forgot and started his walk into the adjoining room. He had felt his legs and responded by thinking he could walk. However, he was jolted into reality as he proceeded to get out of bed. The subconscious mind cannot differentiate the real from the imagined. That is a very important concept! I will repeat it. The subconscious mind cannot tell the difference between the imagined and the real. Can you think of the positive and negative implications of this great idea? We are influenced by whatever we tell our mind, whether it is true or not. We can tell it over and over again that we are not good at math, lousy athletically, or physically ugly and the mind will accept whatever we tell it. We can tell it that we find life to be wonderfully educational, that we are getting better at arithmetic, or that we have a pleasing personality and the same mind will accept it.

Each of us are constantly feeding the subconscious with our internal dialogue or self-talk. It is either elevating our perception of life or feeding our operating system (the brain) with information which distracts from a happy, progressive, and developmental existence. If our self-talk centers around ideas and thoughts like: "I can't remember names," "I'm a klutz," "It's no use," "It's going to be one of those days!," "I'm just no good at this," and "With my luck I'll never make it," then life is going to produce results from this self-defeating junk. Please understand, I know that all of us come into life with different talents, special capacities, and even limitations. I am not suggesting that if we simply say over and over again, "I am a world-class gymnast, I am a world-class gymnast, I am a world-class gymnast, I am a world-class gymnast ... ," then we will be competing in the next Olympics. I know we have different capacities, body types, intelligence, and genetics. However, the day any one of us buys into, accepts, and internalizes that we cannot stand on our hands, tumble, do a somersault, or learn to at least balance ourselves on a four inch wide beam for thirty seconds, is the day we will begin to demonstrate the same. EVERYTHING IN OUR LIVES BEGINS, CONTINUES, AND ENDS WITH THE WAY WE TALK TO OURSELVES!

When we learn to replace our self-talk or internal dialogue with "I think I can's," "Let me try, I have a feeling I can learn," "I am healthy and am beginning to feel much better," "Nothing can stop me now," "I like who I am," "I can do better, it's not like me to forget," "I am organized and have a sense of direction in my life," "I enjoy my relationships," "Understanding and being tolerant of others is one of my greatest assets," "I am learning to respect myself more and more each day," and "I win my private victories"—life has a way of following the channel toward those kinds of results.

Proactive Operating Process (P.O.P.)

Since we are already using the statements "It's like me" or "It's not like me" in our internal dialogue or self-talk, let's examine how we might be able to harness them in moving us toward a more progressive life. To be proactive means to be responsible for our own lives. Our behavior is a function of our decisions. We must take the initiative and choose what our internal dialogue will be. If we do not choose and assume full responsibility for what we think about and talk about to ourselves, then the Law of Entropy will allow us to slip slowly but very surely into a self-talk script which will not move us toward the fulfillment of our greatest capacities. We can do something about our self-talk scripts.

The process has many names, we will use the acronym "POP." The Proactive Operating Process is an exercise where you can harness your self-talk dialogue "It's like me" or "It's not like me" to change behavior. Let's assume for a moment that you are one who has a habit of being late to meetings or is always running just a little behind on meeting deadlines or commitments. You don't like the feeling that comes from this habit and you would like to change it. First, write down a positive phrase which reads something like "I am always on time in completing my commitments and arriving at meetings." Read and repeat this several times each day. Now, when you go to a meeting and you find that your old habit pops up its ugly head and you arrive late to the gathering, take a deep breath and as you walk into the room say out loud, (this takes a little courage) "Excuse me, IT'S NOT LIKE ME TO BE LATE." Make sure you say it out loud and announce it to those already there. There is a good chance those who know you best will roll their eyes and mutter an expletive or two but that's okay. Now, in all future meetings or when you complete a commitment on time, say to yourself quietly and confidently, "IT'S LIKE ME TO BE ON TIME." Enjoy the feelings you have when you do it and say it. If you will focus your attention on the POP technique of first changing your self talk and altering your behavior, you will notice in fifteen to twenty-one days that you are arriving on time more often to meetings and are more timely in completing your commitments. I have noted in my own life and have testimonies of many who have reduced stress, brought down their golf score, and increased their enjoyment of life with giving a little attention to the way they talk to themselves. Remember, your subconscious mind cannot tell the difference between the imagined and the real. My friend could not tell that he didn't have legs when he left it up to his feelings. Our subconscious minds will believe anything we tell it. If we practice feeding it affirmative and positive messages via our internal dialogue (self-talk), we will find that feelings and associated behavior change. Try it!

The Art of Positive Vision

Buddha said "All that we are is the result of what we have thought." Emerson added "The ancestor of every action is thought." Wise King Solomon taught that "As a man thinketh, so is he." Modern day motivator Napoleon Hill promised, "Whatever the mind can conceive and believe it can achieve." One of my favorites was taught by Boyd K. Packer when he said "Whatever you play on the stage of your mind, is a preview of a coming attraction." There is tremendous power in understanding and employing the art of positive vision.

When you think about it, everything is created twice. First, in the mind and second literally. When the architect conceives and idea of a home he wants to design, he first sees it as an impression in the mind. When a quarterback calls a play in the huddle or when he is calling the signals at the line of scrimmage, he sees and passes on a mental image to the other players on the team of who they should block, where they should run, and the pattern on the field that will be executed. When we want a drink of water, our brain receives an image of what we want, where to go to find a cup, where we must walk to find a faucet or dispenser of water, and etc. Every dimension of our lives is created twice. What you and I "play on the stage of our minds is a preview of a coming attraction." There is no question about it!

So the question is, what aew we thinking about? What dominates our vision? Do we see actions that lead to successful results and outcomes, or do we see ourselves doing dumb things, making shortsighted choices, and never being in the winners' circle for anything.

There is a great story told about one of baseball's greats, Warren Spawn. The details of the story escape me, but the essence was that in the final game of the World Series he was pitching his team to a victory. However, in the final inning with his team leading only by one, he was pitching to a prolific batter who, if allowed a hit with runners on base, could turn the game and the series into a loss. Warren was very good at taking directions from his catcher. He therefore, looked at his catcher, for the signal of what kind of pitch to deliver. The manager near the dugout also saw the catchers signal and stopped the game to have a conference on the mound. "Dumb strategy, catcher!" the manager scolded. "You know that this batter hits a great high inside pitch, why did you signal Warren to pitch a high inside ball?" Without listening to the response he blurted out angrily, "Do not throw a high inside pitch. He will hit the ball out of the park and we will lose the series ... got that Warren? Do not throw a high inside pitch!" The manager went back toward the dugout, the catcher back to his position behind the plate, and Warren Spawn prepared to deliver one of the most important pitches in his career, at least one of the most watched. What was flashing in his mind? "Do Not Throw a High Inside Pitch ... Do Not Throw a High Inside Pitch ... Do Not Throw a High Inside Pitch ... He will knock the ball out of the park, we will lose the series ... Do Not Throw a High Inside Pitch." With such bright and flashing messages dominating his VISION, Warren Spawn wound up and delivered the critical pitch. You know the rest of the story and history tells the outcome of that game. The ball went high inside, the batter hit the ball out of the park for a home run, and the old Milwaukee Braves lost the series.

What kind of vision do we embrace when we focus on the reverse of what we want to achieve? Think about it. How have we learned to communicate? "Don't be late," "Don't forget," "Don't spill the milk," "Don't .. . Don't ... Don't." A colleague once said, "We would never ever give instructions to a three year old child by saying, `Do not go over there by the table and get one

---

of those chairs and pull it across the room and put it right here ... right here by this cupboard ... and don't get up on the cabinet top here and reach up and get the jar of beans that is up there on the top shelf ... do you understand? Don't you do that! And most of all, don't get that jar down and take any of those beans out of the jar and don't you dare put those beans up your nose!'" My colleague was right, we wouldn't give instructions to a three-year old like that. Yet today in American Schools, it is estimated that by ten o'clock each day after just a couple of hours of class time, the average elementary student hears scores of negative vision statements from their teachers i.e., "don't do it this way or that way," "don't run," "don't talk," "don't forget," etc.

What would happen if we made an effort to change the way we communicate so that our statements promoted positive vision instead of negative vision? Maybe our communications to self and others could look more like: "Remember to be a few minutes early," "You are always so good to remember to complete your work," "Here, let's put the glass of milk right here in front of your plate so it won't spill."

While the Art of Positive Vision can be observed in every arena of life, it is often most easily observed in the field of athletics. We can see gymnasts standing in position ready to initiate their routine and playing in their mind each component part before they proceed to the mat, the bar, or the balance beam. We can see skillful basketball players standing at the free throw line mentally going through the motion of shooting and making their shot before the referee even hands them the ball. We can see high jumpers preparing to jump by seeing themselves go toward the bar, going off the right foot, elevating the opposite leg, and clearing the bar with some ease prior to their even starting their run.

Perhaps you know where some of our greatest research and insights came from. Years ago, long before the unification of Germany and the democratization of the Soviet Union, many were puzzled at why the Soviet and East German athletes performed so much better in international competition than the USA, Japan, and other nations so focused on athleticism. Why did these two countries garner so many of the medals in the Olympic Games? Maybe we could understand Russia, but little tiny East Germany was a real mystery. We sought to blame it on "quasi professionalism" or steroids, or some deviant external benefits they had that others didn't have. Then defectors from Soviet and East German teams began to give us some of the answers.

The Soviet and East German athletes were being coached and taught via a method called "Autogenic Conditioning." The majority of their practice time was not conducted on the playing field or floor mat. They were practicing mentally. They were rehearsing over and over again in the minds eye. Their actual practice was actually just an opportunity to exhibit what they had vividly rehearsed hundreds of times mentally. Once practiced and perfected in the mind, they physically completed the routine then mentally rehearsed the routine making finite corrections and improvements.

In his insightful book *Psycho-Cybernetics,* Dr. Maxwell Maltz, a world re-nowned plastic surgeon, gives us some excellent information that supports the mental rehearsal notion. I quote from Dr. Maltz's book, "Realizing that our actions, feelings and behavior are the result of our own images and be-liefs gives us the lever that psychology has always needed for changing per-sonality."

It opens a new psychologic door to gaining skill, success, and happiness.

Mental pictures offer us an opportunity to "practice" new traits and attitudes, which otherwise we could not do. This is possible because again—your nervous system cannot tell the difference between an actual experience and one that is vividly imagined.

If we visualize ourselves performing in a certain manner, our system accepts it nearly the same as having the actual experience. Mental practice helps to make perfect.

In a controlled experiment, psychologist R. A. Vandell proved that mental practice in throwing darts at a target, improves aim as much as actually throwing the darts. In the study—everyday for a period of time, the person sat in front of the target and imagined perfect aim.

Dr. Maltz also refers to a report given by *Research Quarterly* where an ex-periment was conducted to verify the effects of mental practice on improving skill in making basketball free throws. One group of one hundred students actually came to the gym and practiced shooting the ball for half an hour every day for twenty days. They were scored on the first and last days.

A second group of one hundred students was scored on the first and last days and engaged in no practice in between.

A third group of one hundred was scored on the first and last day, then spent twenty to thirty minutes each day outside the gym in a relaxed environment, imagining that they were shooting the ball at the hoop.

The first group, which actually practiced twenty minutes every day, improved in scoring twenty-four percent. The second group had no improvement. The third group, which practiced in their imaginations, improved in scoring by twenty-three percent.

In another unpublished study, the exact same variables were recreated with one exception, the third group was actually brought into the gym and each stood at the free throw line and mentally practiced shooting the ball to the hoop for five minutes. They were instructed to imagine seeing the ball leave their hand go to the hoop and swish through the net. They were to repeat this action over and over again during the five minute period. Then they were asked to go to the bleachers or stand and see themselves at the line shooting. They imagined seeing themselves as a spectator would standing at the line with perfect form and stance. They were instructed to see themselves in slow motion shooting a perfect free throw, over and over again for five minutes. Then they were sent back to the line to shoot another five minutes of imaginary shots, never even touching a real basketball. They completed this exercise for twenty days.

Again all three groups were tested at the conclusion of this study. Again the first group improved at about twenty-five per cent. Group two had no negligible improvement at all. The third group improved nearly ten percentage points better than those who actually shot the ball in their practice. Why? The first group was hampered by the actual realization of missing about every fifth or sixth shot. The third group had a three-week diet of seeing themselves and experiencing only making the shot ... never missing! In all actuality when they were given the ball to shoot they did miss, but the focus of this study was on the level of improvement in just twenty days by individuals who "mentally practiced" performance.

This idea is exciting to me. Consider both the positive and negative implications of it. Since the human brain and nervous system are engineered so that mental creations have an enormous impact on actual behavior, we can practice our performance within the mental imagining system and improve our behaviors. We can enhance the quality of our lives by being a controlled daydreamer. Unfortunately it also means that if we allow ourselves to mentally rehearse negative behaviors, we will reap the reward of doing so.

The Law of Entropy again raises its heartless head and reminds us that "our vision, unattended or neglected will naturally move toward an undifferentiated state." Simply, if we don't pay attention to what we are thinking and envisioning, the negative input from the environment will ultimately take over and we will imagine negative results and also reap them.

Everything is created twice! Once in our minds eye, and then we proceed to tangibly replay what we have mentally created. Yes, I think Buddha was right when he said "All that we are is the result of what we have thought." Emerson was right on target when he reminded us that "the ancestor of every action is thought." Simply and sweetly stated in the wisdom of one who had a unique capacity to synthesize truth, Solomon's message is instructive, "As a man thinketh, so is he." I have come to appreciate the elevating notion given by Napoleon Hill that "whatever the mind can conceive and believe it can achieve." I endorse and personally embrace the truth found in the words of Boyd K. Packer when he said "Whatever you play on the stage of your mind is a preview of a coming attraction."

The Art of Positive Vision is a learnable skill worth paying attention to. It could be the difference between common outcomes in our lives and extraordinary success in our endeavors. This is not some kind of PMA (Positive Mental Attitude) hoopla nor is it an exercise in new age cure-all's. The Art of Positive Vision is as old and real as its roots which are deeply found in a simple truth called "Faith."

Summary

Several years ago, a man initiated a change in my life which took about forty-five seconds. Long before I ever heard of the word paradigm or had even a glimpse of expectation theory, this wonderful human being took less than a minute of his valuable time and planted a few seeds which have brought me a blessed harvest. I was cut from my tenth grade high school basketball team. My expectations were shattered! I was one of the fifty losers who didn't make it. I did not measure up to the expectations of significant adults in my life. In my young mind, I was a loser! In an effort to mend my broken heart, my Dad suggested I could play in the league sponsored by our church for boys fourteen through eighteen years old. I was not comforted by that suggestion! I didn't want to play church basketball, I wanted to play high school varsity basketball, be one of the best, make the All-State Team, get a college scholarship, and maybe even play in the NBA. Church basketball leagues in my mind at that tender age were for losers who couldn't make it where the crowds gather and fans cheer. While I can now see the error of my paradigm or belief, it was none the less the way I saw it then. My father's encouragement did not make me feel any better but I concluded that to play church ball was better than not playing at all. It was then that I came to know the man that would change my paradigm and indirectly many of the outcomes that have blessed my life.

His name was Frank Palmer. He was my church team coach. While he knew the game of basketball better than the school coaches, I didn't realize until years later that he more importantly understood that boys were embryonic men waiting to discover themselves. He understood that careless shouting at a young player may change some immediate behavior but has the capacity to scar his image of himself and who he becomes both on and off the court.

One day after we had practiced for about an hour, he closed the practice session and instructed us to shower and prepare to leave. I lingered on and continued to shoot the ball while my friends cleaned up and made ready to leave the gym. Everyone, including Coach Palmer, vacated the gym and went downstairs into a dressing/shower room. All alone I shot for five or ten minutes in the large vacant gym. Then I saw Frank walk through the gym door and stop just inside. I could see him from the corner of my eye, but pretended not to notice him. He was standing with his arms folded watching me rather intently. I continued to shoot the basketball three or four times, spanning all of about fifteen seconds. Then he moved closer to me on the floor and said "Hey Dave, would you repeat that jump shot you just did?" Nervously, I complied remembering in my mind's eye, I was a loser and an adult was just about to criticize me and tell me why I was cut from my high school team. I turned, set my feet, went straight up in the air and shot the ball. I don't remember whether it went in the hoop or not. I do remember what Frank said to me though. He said "David, do you know who you remind me of when you shoot that jump shot? ... You look just like Melvin Daniels." (You may not know who Mel was, but I did. He was a great University of New Mexico player who went on to play with NBA's Indiana Pacers). "You do," he said "the way you turn, go straight up and shoot, especially your wrist action, you look just like Mel Daniels." Then Frank turned and walked away leaving me alone again in the gym. No, I'm now pretty sure I wasn't alone. It was me, my ball, and my buddy Mel! How do you think I felt after Frank walked out? What shot do you think I practiced over and over? What new self talk script do you think I accepted and uttered for the next twenty-five years? How do you think I saw myself when one of the significant adults in my life gave me permission to play like Mel? You must know, that I now know that Frank told one of the greatest lies ever uttered, especially inside of a dedicated church gymnasium. However, my subconscious mind couldn't tell the difference between the imagined and the real. Everything in my life began, has continued, and will end with the way I talk to myself. Even lies! Did that experience make any real difference in my life? Well, I didn't make it to the NBA, but I did make my high school team the next two years, played in our state all-star game, and received a scholarship to play college basketball. I still play "noon hoop" (a time around noon everyday when old basketball "has-beens" get together and play basketball for an hour) twenty-five years later and have enjoyed a lot of years of the game. The real reward is seeing how a common insightful man changed my game, and in many ways my life all in about forty-five seconds! The Law of Expectation is real. The Arts of Positive Self-Talk and Vision are just as real and attainable. It is easy to see how the transitions in your life are impacted by these important concepts. Let's be reminded of the purpose of this book and our joint efforts to create a successful tomorrow which lies on the other side of any transition. The purpose is "development," "transformation," and "realignment" in the changes of our lives. What you think about, talk to yourself about, dream about, and anticipate with confidence will make a difference in what you find on the other side of "change."

We will draw upon our understanding of this fundamental law and these two arts in a future assignment. I hope that you will deeply consider the impact of your self-talk and what kind of mental imaging habits you have allowed into your life.

Chapter Nine

BALANCE

I once observed a mime playing with six sticks and a stack of ceramic plates. He began by placing one stick vertically into a static stand on the floor. He tried to balance one of the twelve-inch plates on the upper point of the stick. It obviously would not stay balanced and fell to the floor breaking into several pieces. He took another plate and attempted again to set the plate on the top of the stick. Again it fell to the ground and broke into pieces. Sadly, the mime puzzled over the dilemma. He looked up and down the stick and then examined one of the ceramic plates for several seconds, then smiled boldly to the onlooking crowd. He took a plate, laid it on top of the stick as he had done before, this time carefully placing the point of the stick in the center of the plate. Then he began to spin the plate. Faster and faster he spun it, until the plate would stay on top of the stick for nearly a minute. The crowd cheered! While the mime bowed and was obviously enjoying the accolades, the spinning plate slowed down, began to wobble, and finally crashed to the floor. The crowd laughed and the frowning mime started to leave the stage with embarrassment, paused, then came back to the center of the stage signaling to the crowd that he had a solution. He proceeded to set up one, then two, and finally a total of six vertical sticks spaced across the stage about four feet apart. He swept the broken ceramic into a little pile at the back of the stage. Taking one new plate, he placed it on the point of the first stick as he had done before, and began spinning it until it independently maintained its own balance. Quickly he took another plate and stuck it on top of the second stick and brought it to an independent spin. Before picking up a third plate he directed his attention back to the first one and brought it back to a strong independent spin, and then just a tap or two on the second plate. He put a third plate on its stick, got it spinning, then added spinning touches to plates one and two for just a brief moment, and then a touch or two on the third plate. Again he added a fourth plate and went through the same routine until he had established six spinning plates. He would walk past the spinning plates and give a spinning touch or two to each. He successfully maintained the six spinning plates for several minutes by giving each just moment of attention. The crowd applauded. Again as the mime's attention was directed toward the applause he failed to pay appropriate attention to the spinning ceramic disks. The plate on stick four began to wobble and the crowd laughingly directed the mime's attention to it just as it fell to the floor and broke. He quickly took another plate, placed it on stick four and began to spend the necessary time getting it to independent spinning status. While directing his attention to the new plate, first one and then two and soon all of the other plates began to wobble, vacillate, and move unsteadily. The frowning mime frantically tried to salvage his meritorious feat by paying attention to the teetering platters. However it was all in vain. Finally in turn, each plate crashed to the floor while the crowd laughed.

Two stagehands ran onto the platform and swept the broken ceramic to the pile at the back of the stage. They then added six more sticks, making a total of twelve. The audience watched as the mime went through the same process as before until he had twelve spinning platters, maintaining each by paying just momentary but focused individual attention. The crowd stood and clapped until the curtains drew shut and the act ended.

The entire scene took nearly fifteen minutes. That seems to be a lengthy time, but the audience was glued to the mime's performance and never seemed to tire of his presentation. Why could an impersonate comedian maintain the attention of his crowd for such a long period of time? I wonder if it isn't because we all relate so well to the mimicry of trying so desperately to maintain and pay attention to many roles and values at the same time. We all identify with the struggle with having one or more of our plates begin to wobble, and feel how relentless it is to keep renewed effort into putting it back into orbital balance while another plate or two begin to show the effects of neglect.

For me the message of the mime was that if I will focus, even a little time each day to each role or value in my life, I can successfully do a lot of things while maintaining a balance. However, if I start focusing a disproportionate amount of time to one "plate," neglecting the others, they will start screaming for my attention almost in unison and my capacity to give remedial response is diminished.

The Law of Balance

The Law of Balance is about harmony. It suggests that harmony in one's life promotes progression, flexibility, and inner peace. Dr. M. Scott Peck, in his best selling book, *The Road Less Traveled* says "Balancing is the discipline that gives us flexibility. Extraordinary flexibility is required for successful living in all spheres of activity. Balancing is a discipline precisely because the act of giving something up is painful—however the *loss* of balance is ultimately more painful than the giving up required to maintain it. Think of that in light of the mime and the spinning plates. Balancing is a discipline because it requires that we not get distracted by cheering audiences or by our own sense of pride. If we allow such to occur, the loss of balance (multiple teetering platters) is ultimately more painful than the giving up required to maintain it. Balance is so easy to talk about and yet so hard to maintain. There is something about human beings, particularly in our present society, that fosters our moving out of harmony and the loss of equilibrium. The seducing characteristic of being out of balance is that it is usually masked and undetected by our own senses until a crisis happens to give us a proverbial "wake-up call."

So why is balance so critical to a happy life? Why are flexibility and harmony precursors to inner peace? Remember, laws don't care. That is just the way it is. We can observe the clues generated by people around us who do maintain a sense of balance in their lives. They are able to adapt to change better than others. Their self-esteem is appropriately high, and they exhibit a love for living. While the Law of Opportunity gives them "more to do than time to do it," the inner peace and harmony they enjoy produces some special ability to stay focused and give the issues which matter most, ordinate priority. Likewise, the Law of Entropy, which simply dictates "each dimension of life unattended or neglected naturally moves to an unorganized, undifferentiated state," is their friend. They pay attention to each "plate" and give it appropriate periodic regard. If we were able to somehow magically adjust our FM radio tuner into the self-talk or tap a microtransmission device into the mental vision system of the balanced person, we would note that they expect to be in balance and somehow their dreams and internal dialogue produce like results. We ourselves know what it feels like to be in balance.

It is also safe to say that we all know how it feels to be out of balance. In fact, chances are significant that our transitions were produced by the nagging sense of imbalance. We may have felt one or more "plates" out of balance and sensed a need to make a change in our lives.

Whether or not your transitions are born in the crucible of disproportion of being out-of-balance or whether you are just arriving at a new chapter in your experience, the Law of Balance will lay its claim on your life. We must all come face-to-face with it and do something about it. If we are to experience the developmental rewards in our transformation and realignment quest in times of change, we must ask ourselves important questions about balance and have the courage to do something about the answers.

Life's Five Core Dimensions

Let's first look at the critical dimensions. In order to live a sustained happy and meaningful life, each person must pay attention to five critical areas: Spiritual, Physical, Educational, Social, and Familial. These are the *core* areas of life which are the heart of everything that matters. You will note that Financial and Professional areas are not included, yet perhaps should be. The reason I have intentionally left them out, has to do with my experience in other lands and cultures. I am of the opinion that the financial and professional "plates" are fabricated by the mind of the individual and are not normally included in the *core* areas. For example, as I have lived and traveled in other countries, I have observed "balanced" happy people with incredible harmony and inner peace who have minimal accumulation of anything material or financial. I have observed the same in the industrialized nations, especially America, where people who are not caught in the snare of unquenchable desire for toys and trappings, are often more happy than those who are. *Yes,* I completely and totally acknowledge the need for financial well-being and having enough money to meet the basic human needs of food, shelter, and education. However, in my opinion, it is the inclusion of this dimension in our lives that is the biggest culprit in throwing our lives out of balance. Does that make sense? The most insidious saboteur of our balance *is* what some term "The Psychology of More"—an attitude that is developed which requires more and more financial accumulation. In fact, if we look at the clues generated by those who are out of balance, high percentages will evidence that the inordinate attention being paid to the financial "plate" is the very reason the others wobble and then crash to the floor. Yet, the most balanced people enjoying the greatest sense of inner peace in their lives may or may not have wealth or anything more than their basic financial needs being met. In short, as someone once said, "enough *is* an attitude, not an amount."

The professional dimension of life is similar. It is intentionally omitted from the *core* because it *is* a way we spend time to receive the above compensation. Neither professional status or wealth dictate harmony and inner peace any more than hyperventilating produces more life. I have observed that harmony and inner peace has little to do with whether a person *is* a teacher, lawyer, or common laborer. Inner peace and harmony seem to come from the *core* dimensions.

If you feel otherwise, I invite you to include one or the other in your *core* group of dimensions. I have chosen to leave them out on the basis that money and doing something to receive that money are as much a part of life as breathing or eating. I must do both to live. Harmony, inner peace, and the flexibility that is produced by being in balance come from being in a state of equilibrium with the *core*. Regardless of WHAT we are (our financial status or professional competency), harmony and inner peace come more from a sense of WHO we are and how we relate to life. WHO we are is a direct result of how we deal with the *core* areas. Let's look at the *core*.

Spiritual

Abraham Maslow states, "Practically everything that happens in the peak experiences, naturalistic though they are, could be listed under the heading of religious happenings." Religious happenings are not denominational or about church. They are happenings that edify the inner self. It *is* knowing and acting upon the deep understanding that human beings are more than a physical body. It is understanding what one insightful person once suggested when he said, "We are not human beings having a spiritual experience, but rather spiritual beings having a human experience." We are more than the body we spend so much time washing, feeding, adorning, making fragrant. We are more than bones, muscles, organs, blood vessels, skin, tendons, and connective tissue. That *is* only the package for the real us. The real you and me are the feelings, attitudes, and emotions which are invisible and intangible.

The Spiritual Dimension sets a capstone on living. It is our personal need to identify who we are, how we fit, and how we relate to others. It is a force greater than ourselves and the universe. Maslow wisely taught that the "peak experiences" are found in our search for and discovery of the real us. These "religious happenings" are the meaningful moments in the feeding and growing of that invisible part of us which constitutes who we are, not just what our package or body looks like. It is learning to run our lives by the real self not merely by the hormones and appetites produced by our package, the body. It *is* learning to put off what one great man called "the natural man" (body, hormones, and cravings) to the end that we elevate and control our lives by the insights, attitudes, feelings, faith, hope, and understanding of our real selves, the invisible and untouchable us, our Spirits.

Since the Law of Balance teaches the principle of harmony, The Law of Entropy reminds us that we must pay attention, and the Law of the Farm mandates we will harvest what we sow in the appropriate season, perhaps we should ask ourselves some questions about what we can do to feed the Spiritual Dimension of our lives. This is the most personal arena of the five. You will discover and decide how you will best meet this critical capstone of your life.

A list of ideas to consider and employ might include enjoying nature. When we resided in Arizona, I enjoyed nature with an early morning walk, observing the rising sun against the Superstition Mountains while considering important questions and discovering their answers about who I was. In Michigan, it was sitting by a small lake in a wooded area, watching geese fly in formation across the northeastern sky, and contemplating my new beginnings and transitional goals. In Idaho, it was climbing a mountain or viewing cascading waterfalls while considering the many good things I enjoy and developing a greater attitude of gratitude. In Florida, it was sitting on a pristine beach, smelling the ocean scents, and taking in the immense psychic space of the seascape.

Such a list might also include getting outside ourselves to serve another without compensation, or perhaps in total anonymity. You may be edified spiritually by reading about happy, successful people who evidence a power to overcome the obstacles of life. Perhaps you are lifted by writing in a personal journal, listening to uplifting music, reading the Bible, enjoying art, meditating, or simply closing your eyes and asking what you can do to contribute in quiet but meaningful ways to the human race, to people you care about, or to the planet earth.

Physical

In recent years, much of global society has begun to pay more attention to fitness related issues. In the United States it was precipitated, in part, by a medical "wake-up call" that we were leading the world in heart disease, cancer, and other critical maladies. While some critics stated it was all a craze or fad, we have seen that it is not. The rise in fitness awareness is here to stay and is a direct response to The Law of Entropy. "Health unattended or neglected will naturally move to sickness, misery, and incapacity." In fact, health is one of those things in life which we must pay attention to—like it or not. I subscribe to a notion of truth that I must take time for my health. I will either voluntarily take the time to maintain it now, or take it later in life, nursing ill health. Either way, I must take time for my health! It is clearly a "pay me now or pay me later" issue. The fact is, we will pay!

How are you doing in the development of your physical dimension? Are you enjoying life with good health or are you frequently lethargic, sick, or unable to perform well at work, school, or recreational pursuits? Sometimes we may be tempted to look past the truth and respond by saying "I am in pretty good health. I am not overweight. My blood pressure is fine, and I don't get many headaches. In fact, my productivity at work is at an all time high. I feel pretty good, or at least I don't get sick." We will want to remember "balance" has some deceptive characteristics. We seldom realize we are moving out of balance until we are out of balance. In other words, we can leave the plate spinning on its own inertia for a while but quietly and deceitfully it will slow down, begin to wobble, and then require an inordinate amount of attention which causes us to lose time and opportunity to spin other plates. Then the whole system of balancing multiple plates becomes a crisis. Sometimes we cannot even detect the wobbling plate until it drops and crashes to the floor. All other plates must then be affected while we spend time renewing our efforts to get it spinning again.

Health is one of those *core* elements which requires overtime attention if symptoms develop, and one may ultimately end up playing catch-up or time-out. Historically, our society has accepted and even promoted a reactive philosophical paradigm. For example, when do people usually call or visit a doctor? With few exceptions, people visit a doctor when symptoms of illness surface when the "health plate" *is* wobbling. What would your doctor say to you if you were to schedule an appointment, and then as you sit with him or her you say something like "Doctor, I feel great! In fact, I feel better than I have felt in a long time. I am here to have you examine me and tell me just how much more healthy I can get and what I should do to improve it." I suspect your doctor would look at you like you are some kind of "nut." Your physician might even recommend that you schedule a visit with a doctor of psychiatry. We have demanded that the wonderful medical profession identify problems and prescribe remedy for "wobbling or broken plates." While I completely acknowledge that runners, walkers, and those who eat right and get plenty of sleep do get sick from time to time, I wonder how different life would be if we were to pay attention to our health and operate from a more proactive paradigm. What would happen if we were to ask ourselves, "what can I do today to be even more healthy than I am or have been," perhaps we would experience more progressive outcomes. The Law of the Farm demands a harvest which would make a difference in the way we live and enjoy life.

Physical health is truly a *core* dimension of life, yet it is important to remember that each of us will "spin the plate" differently, based on our interests and capabilities. Let's suggest some different ways we might want to treat this area of our life. For a starter, we ought to consider a physical, dental, and vision examination. Learn all you can about healthy joints, muscles, or blood. Read about nutrition, sleep, and exercise. Check your cholesterol and blood chemistry levels. Learn about a new sport you would like to enjoy. Establish an exercise or fitness program which meets your interest and current health level. If you hate walking but enjoy swimming, then swim your way to fitness. If you enjoy racquetball or tennis but dislike jogging, then center your program around tennis or racquetball. If you smoke, stop! Learn about biofeedback techniques. Depending on your commitment level, you may want to invite a friend to engage in the program with you. Mutual commitment can help you both maintain your program and build lasting relationships as well.

Educational

Thinking, expanding your knowledge, and growing are both important to living a vital life and they are a neverending process. In my association with college students, I have noted a growing inclination for them to get into an erroneous mindset. Many think they will go to school for four to eight years, receive one or more degrees in a field of their choice, then be done with education and work for the following forty years and get rich. The mindset is false! Anyone who buys into that way of thinking is going to find out, either in a painful moment or an exhilarating instant of discovery, that education is forever. Happy and progressive human beings understand the Law of Entropy as it relates to the mind, which says "our minds unattended or neglected naturally move to an unorganized and undifferentiated state." Entropy will not allow us to put our minds on stop. Education is not only important to a happy, growing, progressive human being, it is critical to surviving professionally in our fast-paced and changing technological environment. One recent study estimates that at current levels of progress and change in industry, last year's college graduates must be willing to be retrained in some dimension of their career up to thirteen times during their work life. Isn't that great? If we won't "spin the plate" on our own, we will be forced to by our professions.

Education, however, is much more than being forced to deal with the latest version of Word Perfect, Qua&o Pro, or how to integrate the most efficient methods of robotics into our fabrication planning. Education has as much to do with the process as it does the outcome. It is using the mind and developing vicarious, if not actual, experience in a multitude of endeavors. Think of it. Via education, you can travel to Europe, Russia, Asia, and Orlando without ever leaving your hometown. You can see *Hamlet* or *Les Miserables* without going to Broadway. You can learn another language, appreciate music, keep abreast of the stock market, learn to write or even write a book, study customer service, learn to sell, learn to buy, learn, learn, learn. It's more an attitude than a skill. It's a thirst to know more, to know better ways, to know why, and to think about how we can be smarter than the previous generations in meeting life's greatest challenges. Learning is growing, developing, and a part of transition.

However, the by-product of this process is not always revolutionary or changing. The residual effect of a growing, healthy, active mind *is* what it does to the person. We are more resourceful, tend to be happier, enjoy life more, and become more substantive, experienced, and confident. The process of educating our minds, improves our capacity to enjoy life. It broadens and enlightens. A wise person once said, "We must not cease from exploration and the end of all our exploring will be to arrive where we began and to know the place for the first time." Learning is perpetually fresh and the process is the key to happy living.

Perhaps Ethel Barrymore said it best, "You must learn day by day, year by year to broaden your horizon. The more things you love, the more you are interested in, the more you enjoy, the more you are indignant about—the more you have left when anything happens."

How are you doing in the educational area of your life? Like health and fitness, you can mesmerize yourself into thinking you are all right in this area until you wake up and realize that the routine and boredom of life has replaced fun and enjoyment. You wake up and life is a drag. Consider ways that you can proactively get yourself engaged in educational activity. Take a class or identify a new hobby. Maybe you should consider learning about organic gardening, salt water aquariums, birds, or wood finishing. In our shrinking world, maybe a second language would not only stimulate your mind but make you a more valuable asset in your professional arena. If you have two languages, why not a third? Read a book, listen to audio tapes, or visit the Orient, Switzerland, or Cuba by checking out the video section of your library. Find out if there are any satellite "live" video educational transmissions to your library.

Most people in transition find this dimension a critical stepping stone in the quest for change, development, and realignment. Students, or those changing professions, and persons looking back on lost or fractured relationships are all typically focused on learning how to make positive changes. Regardless of where you are, decide now to include education as a part of the rest of your life. Start "spinning this plate" and giving it appropriate attention for the rest of your life. You will come to understand more fully why it is *core* to a happy vital life.

Social

The social area of our lives is one of the most interesting to consider. Just how important are other people in our happiness? Can we live productively without other people? If you lived in a vacuum or alone on some deserted island over time, what would be important to you? Would you care about how much money you made, how big your house was, or where you worked? What would life be like for days, years, decades, or a lifetime if you didn't have someone to share it with? Do you know any truly happy and successful people who are alone? The history books are full of stories of human beings who lived without any significant social element in their lives and ultimately died from self inflicted wounds or simply stopped living. People make life worth living! They also can make it frustrating, can't they? People make the difference whether life is dull or fun, happy or sad, vital or boring. While we all maintain full responsibility for how we encounter life, including the actions of others, we would all agree that people make life. People are life!

Emerson penned the following true thought, "We take care of our health, we lay up money; we make our roof tight and our clothing sufficient, but who provides wisely that he shall not be wanting in the best property of all— friends." Tennyson added this insightful thought, "I am a part of all I have met."

People are life! What do you know about others? We must ask ourselves what we need to learn about dealing with others, enhancing relationships, and being more ourselves for others to enjoy. As we consider this *core* dimension perhaps it would be well to inventory how well we are "spinning this plate." We will find that the Laws of Entropy, the Farm, Opportunity, and even Expectation raise their heads again within this fundamental dimension of life. Entropy reminds me that "relationships unattended or neglected will naturally move toward an unorganized, undifferentiated state." If we don't pay attention to our relationships, spend time and cultivate what we have built with others, they will go away! "Life produces more to do than time to do it" says the Law of Opportunity. Since we do what we value the most, we must put people and relationships somewhere in the front of the line and give appropriate attention to people and relationship issues. Expectation of what a relationship can be is the first step to having a great one. The Law of the Farm or Harvest promises if we do pay attention, cultivate, irrigate, and pay the daily price we will have a rich rewarding harvest.

What are you doing about the social part of your life? Perhaps you can create and maintain a list of people you know which you would like to keep in touch with. If you are not prone to write letters, then use the telephone, but keep in touch! Pick up the telephone today and talk to someone you appreciate who you haven't communicated with for some time. Note how you feel after you hang up the telephone. There *is* a message in that feeling!

Maybe you should take a class or read about communication skills. Maybe you should make it a point to meet someone new today. Go fishing, to a ball game, an opera, a movie, a race, or on a walk with someone. Remember, we do what we value the most, so you need to schedule it or just go today and do it. Notice how you feel when you return. I predict you will like yourself much better, your friend's day will be richer, and all those things you just had to get done today will find a way to be done tomorrow and life will go on ... just a little richer and fuller.

Family

It is possible that the cornerstone to all which is truly meaningful in life revolves around society's basic unit, the family. It is the basis of tomorrow and is at the root of our societal *success* or failure today. Dr. Pearsall has said, "No matter what the form of your family, from single parent household to the largest multi-generation family in town, your work at keeping families together is the job of saving our world.... I warn you that if your family does not come first your family will not last." Maintaining balance by "spinning this plate" is critical to the quality of harmony which will promote high levels of productivity and inner peace in our lives.

I find great enjoyment watching people. As I travel around this great country and spend a lot of time in airports, I delight in observing people coming and going. You can always *see* a spouse and frequently children escorting a loved one to the gate as they depart for a business related venture in some distant city. You see middle-aged children taking their aging parents to the airport to send them home after a visit. The quiet observer can hear tearful good-byes and tender joyous moments of reunion, hugs, kisses, smiles, and love as families come and go.

Why is it that life's most memorable holiday experiences revolve around family? Christmas has its warmth of wide-eyed children excitedly waiting for the days cheer and enjoyment. Thanksgiving turkey and extended families gather around an expanded dining table with the smell of home cooked fare. Valentine's Day, Mother's Day, Father's Day, and Hanukkah are others. Why is it that memories of family vacations, visits from Grandpa and Grandma, and being with cousins bring happiness to our inner person? Have you ever watched a new father coming from the delivery room of the hospital or observed a mother holding her newborn child? Why is it that families provide so much joy?

Why too, are life's most difficult trials tied to family concerns? You, the reader, may be one who has none of the above mentioned memories or joys. Perhaps you know someone whose life has revolved around broken relationships, divorce, sibling rivalry, family fights, feuds between adult family members, bitterness toward an unfaithful spouse, generation gaps, incest, abuse, and other tragic parent-child abnormalities. The most difficult of life's challenges rest or find their beginnings in the irregular relationships within the family circle.

Balancing this cornerstone component of life takes pure and focused attention. The Law of Entropy again reminds us that "family unattended or neglected will naturally move toward chaotic, fractured relationships, and the kind of outcomes which burden society instead of bless it." I have found that when I am paying attention, real and conscious attention, to this area of my life, everything else in the long term seems to work out just fine. In those moments when life has dealt its unyielding blows, and the dragons have been almost harder to fight than I could bear, I have been able to find solace

---

within the walls of my home and with people I call family. However, that solace and comfort which has come from a family who I herald as my "best friends," has a price! It takes time, energy, and attention that is sometimes hard to give. It takes both planned and calculated attention along with an alertness for the golden moments when spontaneous response brings the greatest rewards. My wife and I determined prior to our vows at the altar that we would pay attention to our marriage, continue our courtship after the honeymoon bliss had lost its luster, and learn how to become best friends forever. We also discussed and planned for our children with an eye to building relationships with each one of them. We have a long way to go and a lot more to learn, but I have concluded through a rather non-scientific observation, that a child's FUN-BAROMETER is at its highest when they are playing and laughing with their dad and joking with their mother. For that reason, it is no mistake that each home we've lived in has been equipped with a large round trampoline in the backyard—even at the expense of grocery money or the finest line of living room furniture. Each time we have moved into a new home we've surveyed the yard together for a place where we would level, pour ten cubic yards of concrete, and finish it into a basketball court. Do you have any idea how much concrete costs? Perhaps a better question might be, "Do you have any idea what the dividend pay-off has been so far, from the hours of silly jumping and playing on the trampoline with my children ... or how important the moments when we've laid together at night with our backs on the jumping mat looking into the star-filled sky talking about important things ... or how the return on our investment in a few cubic yards of finished concrete has made our family life rich with memories of shooting basketballs while talking about goals and ambitions, about what to do with new and raging hormones that arrive unannounced in a teenager's life, and improving the "D" on the last report card with a grade more consistent for a great kid with great potential?

Now, whether you get into trampolines or roller blades or cement basketball courts or walks along the beach or sitting in a booth at your favorite ice cream store or hiking together along wooded paths or looking at the city together from the lofty heights atop a skyscraper ... it doesn't really matter! What will matter is that you make a conscious and calculated effort to create opportunities to build family relationships. Entropy requires that we pay attention. However, be careful not to overstructure your intent and beware if you haven't paid attention to a child or your parents for years. One cannot all of a sudden say, "Here I am ... I am your best friend!" Relationship building is a process and takes time and investment.

Since you are reading this book, chances are you are in or approaching a state of transition or change. You may be looking back on times which have yielded strained or broken relationships. You may be wishing you could start over and build a better relationship from the wisdom of hindsight. Life unfortunately grants no replays. Time gone is time lost. However, we can take heart in knowing as Abraham Lincoln once said, "The best thing about the future is that it comes only one day at a time." We can internalize our understanding of "Carpe Diem," and seize the day today and do something tomorrow to build our family relationships.

If you are a student in the transitions of young adulthood, you cannot change how your parents may have failed to invest into building your life and relationships. However, you can forgive them and decide now to build your philosophy so that your future will produce incredible spousal or child relationships. If you have been fortunate to have excellent experiences in your own family life, then decide now to perpetuate and even improve the outcomes in the future. If you have a strained relationship with your parents, do what you can do to change that. Do something today that will build a better next chapter.

Wherever you are in your family circumstances, take time to consider what you can do better now. Understand that taking time for this dimension of your life is doing something that will make your contribution to saving the world. Remember, it's a day by day process, and like on the farm, it may take a long and nurturing cultivation before it brings results. The important thing is that we do something and do it consistently.

You might consider, from a long list of possibilities, something such as to:

Call a child or your parents on the telephone for an informal chat. Give a compliment or write a "thank you" or note of appreciation to a family member. Go for a walk, play ball, go to the zoo, go for a ride, go shopping at the mall, or play a card game with someone in your family. Plan your next vacation, go to the library, write a letter, send flowers, buy a bag of candy, start a family memory picture book. Maybe you will want to find a book about families or information about understanding another family member. Do something! Do it today!

Summary

There is a trick to spinning multiple plates. There is even a greater trick to doing it so that all stay in perpetual motion and none start their wobbly descent to a crash on the floor. The key to the trick is in paying a few moments of attention in periodic sequence. The trick to having a good, happy, balanced life with a sense of inner peace, is paying consistent periodic attention to the five basic "plates" of life. By doing so, the flexibility produced will allow you to add even more plates and spin them all successfully.

Chapter Ten

THE LAW OF 1%

If a stock broker were to approach us and convince us that we could invest wisely into a New York Stock Exchange offering by giving their company one penny out of every dollar that passes through our individual earnings, and the company would guarantee us ten cents in return every 30 days for the rest of our lives, would you do it? I would! Assuming it was a reasonably good company listed on the New York Exchange, no one would have to beg me to try that investment? Especially, if it is guaranteed. Understanding that one penny out of every dollar is extremely low risk .. . we would have ninety-nine cents from every dollar on which to operate our life. Even if we were to lose our investment and find the claims of the company to be false, the loss would not adversely affect our financial lives.

If I could convince you to invest one per cent of your day, every day, to an exercise which would bring you incredible returns ... would you do it? In other words, would you dedicate one percent of 1440 minutes everyday to an investment which would make more difference in your life than anything else you could do? It means you would need to commit an investment of 14.4 minutes each day to achieving "returns" which would positively increase your effectiveness, development, transformation, realignment, and change. Guaranteed! So, will you do it?

The world doesn't. The masses may give a sporadic five or ten minutes once or twice a week. There is a small percentage of society who will give four or five minutes a day making a "to do" list or thinking about what they should do to become better people, professionals, parents, and so forth. Does that activity and amount of time make a difference? You can be sure it does. It makes a lot of positive difference. It is a rare person in the human family who will give even one-percent of their life to insuring that they are on track, that their daily living is appropriately focused, and that they are tuned-in to their inner guidance system.

There is enough evidence that this personal investment activity performed on a daily, consistent basis results in an important sure return that I call this the "Law of One Percent." Fourteen and a half minutes a day—that's such a small thing! When you consider that everyday we will spend 360 to 480 minutes sleeping, 480 to 600 minutes working, 60 to 90 minutes eating, and if we're average citizens of the United States or Canada, we will mindlessly spend 100 to 200 minutes vegetating in front of a television. Why is it that we will invest more time into making a Christmas gift list, deciding which new car to buy, or scanning the movie section of our local newspaper to determine which movie we will see this week, than we will to building and maintaining a well directed life? In many ways that is a paradoxical question which we may never find the complete answer to, because it is so individual. I do know that when I seriously engage in the process and vow that I will not allow anything to cheat me out of my 14.4 minutes on a daily, consistent basis, the Law mandates a literal return which I can feel as well as see.

This is one of the shortest chapters of this book. Yet the implications of understanding and employing the contents of this chapter may be the most important one. If we understand this Law, learn the "art" or skill associated with employing the law, and then give it a chance to produce by living it, I believe we will experience a change and a difference hitherto unknown. Living this law drives everything else we do. We can create a personal Creed Document, learn how to improve our self talk patterns, and understand the implications of the Law of the Harvest. We can understand ourselves and others better and even improve our relationships. However, when we learn to skillfully employ and enjoy the Law of One Percent, its driving force will produce energizing, self-perpetuating returns which will bless our lives forever.

The Art of Personal Preparation

If we commit to invest one percent of our lives to our lives, then learning the skill of what to do during that time is critical. It's not hard, but it is important, and it is as individual as we are.

In the next chapter of this book we will be formulating the core of your personal Creed Document. We will employ the Art of Positive Self Talk and the Art of Positive Vision into building affirmations with respect to our values. We will create an operating system to rewrite our self talk scripts while giving positive vision to daily living. One of the activities which should be a part of our daily investment of one-percent is reading and pondering those affirmations. You will know how much time to dedicate to this activity, perhaps about one-forth or four minutes of your time every day. Another minute or two could be given to looking at your "balance" quotient; determining if you are giving appropriate attention to spinning each of your plates and maintaining them in such a way that your capacities are increased in each. Another minute or two might be dedicated to reading an inspiring poem, the words of a song, or a quotation which inspires or helps you stay focused. Personally, I make sure that everyday I review one area of my values and affirmations (which takes 3 or 4 minutes). The last three or four minutes of the 14.4 minute block is dedicated to making my daily to do list and considering important action items. The time in between (8 to 10 minutes) is variable. Some days I will, as mentioned above, read a poem, review the words to a song, or ask myself questions about how I am doing with my balance. Other days, I will put on meditative music, sit back and interview myself with regards to my direction, my actions, or my commitments. Music brings something out in people. It has the capacity to stir feelings and influence attitude. Somedays, with the music in the background I will spend the length of a song visualizing myself in some future event, i.e., standing in front of a group giving a presentation ... I can see the faces of the people in my audience, we are connected, they are enjoying the thoughts I am giving, and at the conclusion they express their appreciation will applause ... several come to me afterwards to seek more information and give positive comments about their experience in the encounter. Or sometimes I visualize myself sitting with one of my children laughing or talking about important things ... I sense a special moment where I express to them my love for them and how pleased I am with who they are and what they are becoming. I see a smile come to my child's face and know we are friends. Or I watch myself in wonderful imagery celebrating my upcoming birthday by going to the gym and taking an official size basketball, jumping gracefully, and jamming it (dunking) on a ten foot rim ... I savor the mental moment of doing it in my old age, pretending to hear others in the gym as they comment about my having that unusual ability at my age ... I even imagine the expressions on their faces.

I invite you to do whatever you want during those fifteen minutes, realizing that it is a time to focus, visualize, affirm your goodness, and be introspective by looking inside and privately winning your inner victories.

I am often asked if the best time to make this investment each day is morning, afternoon, or evening. I simply answer "yes." In other words, it doesn't matter so long as you do it every day. I do recommend that you do it at the same time, in the same place, and somewhat in the same way every day. In short, make it a habit! Remember, of all the habits you will ever embrace, and of all the things you will learn from this book or from a dozen others, living this law may be one of the most important driving actions you will ever do, if you do it consistently and with passion.

Chapter Eleven
VALUES IN ACTION

We have created a framework foundation in the previous four chapters which will now allow us to create the keystone to your Creed Document. In our study of The Law of Entropy we are reminded that we must constantly DO something. We must forever pay attention to the direction and character of our lives, or we will naturally move toward an unorganized and undifferentiated human being. We have examined our expectations and understand that "self-talk" scripting and what we play on the stage of our minds are a preview of coming attractions. We have considered the importance of bringing more flexibility to our lives by expanding our capacity to pay attention to balance. Finally, we have come to understand that one of the most important investments we will make in our transitional quest and the habit for maintenance of a progressive life, is found in the Law of One Percent. We are ready to put values into action.

The Power of "Why"

I had the wonderful privilege of growing up in the Northwestern New Mexico town of Farmington. It was a great place to live. I was a member of a Boy Scout Troop and had a great scoutmaster who took us into the enchanting outdoors on a monthly basis. He was particularly gifted with a capacity to tell us stories in a way which activated our minds and caused us to remember important things.

One Friday night around ten o'clock, as we were sitting around a campfire enjoying one of his stories, he stopped and abruptly invited "shhhh! Listen ..." After a few moments he said "nevermind," and continued with his story. About a minute later, again he interrupted his story by commanding "shhhhhhh! Listen!" And again after a few moments he said, "never mind," and continued with his story. Two or three minutes later he stopped his story again and asked us all "Listen. Did you hear that?" Twelve boy scouts turned their ears to the black of the night and listened. "I think I heard the scream of a cougar, a mountain lion. Did any of you?" Then he informed, "Did you guys know that, right through this area, cougars come down from the foothills and go over to the La Plata River, about a mile from here, to drink?" We all sat and listened for the scream of a cougar in the dark of the night with only the flickering light of the fire highlighting our concerned faces. The still of the night was interrupted only by the crackling fire for twenty or thirty seconds. Finally, our leader and story-telling scoutmaster broke the silence by saying, as near as I can recollect, "I had a friend once who was camping out here in these parts of the country and was attacked by a cougar..." he then proceeded to tell us of how his friend was ripped up, bloodied, and barely escaped death from the fangs and claws of the raging animal. As he concluded twelve scouts were huddled a little closer to the fire, each giving a periodic glance over their shoulders into the blackness of the night. We sat silently for a half minute and no one spoke. Our minds were activated and our imaginations running rampant. Our fearless leader then instructed us, "Let's go to bed guys. Hit the sack! Tomorrow we are going to hike over to the river. We need our sleep."

We moved quickly to our tents and climbed into our sleeping bags. Quickly, I strategically placed myself in the middle position of our three-man pup tent. The young scout to my right descended to the bottom of his bag, taking the fetal position and stayed that way for the rest of the night. I have wondered since how he managed to breathe. The fellow scout to my left moved his bag as close to mine as he could, and after getting in, laid on his back, stiff as a board. About every fifteen minutes he would startle me with a question, "Dave, what's that? Did you hear that?" Morning was a long time coming, but finally the night was broken by light in the east. Soon we were up. After breakfast, taking down our tents, and loading the trailer, our scoutmaster huddled us around the front of his van where he had placed a map on the hood for our viewing. He instructed, "I want you guys to hike (one way) over to the La Plata River." He told us that it was only about a mile or two hike to the river and then another mile to our appointed meeting place. He would drive the van to meet us. He identified landmarks on the map and informed us that we would encounter some typical New Mexican sand cliffs preceding a canyon where the river ran. He assured us that although the cliffs were sixty to one hundred feet high, that there were numerous trails which would safely take us to the bottom of the canyon and the river. In the southwestern part of the United States, you can see for long distances. The vistas are seldom shrouded by trees. He told us that from the top of the sand cliffs, we would be able to see the river and the landmark which identified the appointed place to meet. "OK," he said "stick together and hike over. I'll be watching for you and we'll meet in about an hour." We grabbed our canteens and started toward our destination. The most important thing to twelve and thirteen year-old boys anytime you go anywhere is to be first! Most of the boys were nearly running in the direction of the cliffs, canyon, and river.

Within a little while we arrived at the sand cliffs. Sure enough, we could see the river and the landmark meeting place. We walked along the sand cliff looking for the trails our fearless leader had told us we would find to harmlessly take us in our descent. As the others walked forward, I saw a way which appeared to be a "shortcut." It required a ten to twelve foot jump straight down to what then appeared to be a nice trail to the bottom. I lagged behind the others until they rounded a bend in the upper trail and went out of sight. Quickly I scrutinized my option to jump to the trail below which I hoped would be my ticket to reaching bottom first and getting me well ahead of the others in reaching our destination. I positioned myself and jumped safely to the trail. I followed it several feet around a little bend, and then came to a major problem in my strategy. The trail ended abruptly at another significant drop-off into the canyon. It would require an unsafe descent of about sixty feet to the bottom. Wisdom (though I had little at the time) dictated that I backtrack and see if I could catch up with my friends. When I retreated to the cliff I had jumped from moments earlier, I found that getting back up was significantly more challenging than jumping down. In fact I tried and tried to get up that cliff. Finally, I stopped. I was beat! I couldn't get up. I stood there for several minutes trying to decide what to do next. It would be too humiliating for this budding teenager to yell for help and far too vexing to imagine being surrounded by a high level rescue team from the San Juan County Sheriff's Department.

As I stood there thinking of my options, I decided to try again. I could climb up within just a foot or two of making it to the top only to find I could not quite complete the ascent. After another effort or two I stopped and became frightened. I confess in the frustrating realization that I was defeated, this twelve-year-old boy started to tear up and cry. I could imagine what my scoutmaster would say, the lecture I would get from my parents, and finally what would happen if no one missed me. Maybe I would die out there and someone would find my bones months later. In this state of wonder and withdrawal, my mind reeled and rolled with all the negative possibilities. Then, an almost forgotten memory from the night before surfaced ... "cougars"... "blood"... "mountain lions going to the La Plata River to drink"... I approached the cliff again and with more strength, I again made several attempts to climb out of my distress. Still I was defeated in overcoming the final obstacle.

Now my mind was focused less on the cliff and more on the frightful thoughts of large mountain cats, fangs, and the helplessness I felt. I stood firm in the mind-set of "what I should do and how in the world could I do it?" It was then that I heard a rustle in a lone sage brush on a ledge. It was straight above me and slightly to the right of the cliff I had been unsuccessfully trying to negotiate for fifteen minutes. The rustling bush coupled with my imagination did something for me. In fact, within seconds I scrambled and clawed my way to the top and was soon standing out in a small clearing above the sand cliffs. My heart was about to beat out of my chest, and I looked down at my hands to note that the two middle fingernails on both hands were peeled back and bleeding. But I had made it! I had gotten up that cliff which I had unsuccessfully attempted it for over fifteen minutes; I soon realized that the rustle in the sage bush was nothing more than a prairie dog or ground squirrel.

What made the difference? You may be saying, "come on Christensen, don't you know about adrenaline and endorphins? Your body produced the hormonal "shot" to make it up that cliff!" To which I reply, "yes, I know about those things, but what caused the adrenaline to flow?" This is an important point to always remember as we begin to examine and put our values into action. My capacity to perform on that cliff came from the power of "WHY" or the "REASON." When we have enough REASON or WHY in our lives, we can do incredible things. In this case FEAR was the REASON and was a sufficient WHY to increase my capacity to do something I was previously unable to do.

It was several years before I told anyone about that experience. Reflecting on its implications has been important to me. I have learned that when given enough reason, we can accomplish incredible things, however, if we remove the seed of purpose, then the power to act is exploited and diminished to the menial. It is when we forget the real REASON why we work, that it gets boring, unfulfilling, and tends toward a tedious task. When we forget WHY we are in school we slip into just doing what we have to do to complete our assignments and get a grade, rather than learning and growing and gleaning meaningful wisdom. When we forget WHY we are in love, or WHY we are parents, or WHY we build relationships, we slide into the snare of selfishness with concern about how everything effects "me" instead of how much more beautiful the world is when "we" enjoy it together.

The power of values comes when we have a clear sense of, not only, who we are but WHY we are. When we maintain purpose and meaning in our lives, we tend to be able to do wonderful things well. When we live out of a sense of purpose, reason, and why; the "what to do's" and "how to do them's" of our lives also become more focused, directed, and on target. You might say that Values (Reasons, Whys, and Purposes) are the fuel that accelerates us toward living in a way that will produce inner peace and joy.

It is critical for us to understand and remember two important aspects of the relationship between our "actions" and our "values":

1. We will always act in accordance to values in moments of crisis. For example, imagine you are sitting on a beach watching a loved one swim and enjoying playing in the surf, then suddenly a crashing wave drags him under the water pulling him out to sea. You can detect he is experiencing trouble and beginning to drown. You don't puzzle and say to yourself "hmmmm, how much to I value that person? Should I or should I not go out and assist him or even save his life? "You immediately spring to your feet and try to help. Your value of that person automatically spurs you to action, because you place a value on the life of the loved one. We will always act in accordance to our values in crisis moments.

2. When our actions and our values are congruent or come together, we experience a super satisfaction, a joy, or an inner peace. We like ourselves better when we exhibit to ourselves that our actions are completely consistent with the things we value. When we DO what we VALUE we not only do things better, but the residual is a joyful confirming feeling which spawns an even greater capacity to perform.

Understanding these two truths will help us identify and clarify our values, and then create the kind of actions which will be consistent with them. We will live progressively more often and experience the results of doing good things right. We will have more inner peace and joy.

A Beginning

Now we are ready to begin a process to identify and clarify our values and integrate them into our lives through a process of rescripting and vision. Stop for a moment and ask yourself what really matters to you. For what would you be willing to lay your life on the line? In a life or death situation, what person or thing would dominate your attention? Look at it another way... let's assume you have undergone a routine physical examination from your family doctor. In the process the doctor ordered a couple of additional tests, which was your only clue that something might be out of order. Today the doctor calls you to his office and sits you down in a chair across from his. He clears his voice and then speaks, " , I have both good news and bad news. The good news is that you likely will not be bed ridden, sick, or unable to live normally... the bad news is that you have a condition which is both rapid developing and there is no known cure. In short, you can live a life with no restrictions to your physical activity or your capacity to be cerebrally alive. You will do well, however, to understand that the medical profession predicts that unless there is an intervening miracle, you will die within the next six to seven months. No one with this condition has ever lived more than a year after diagnosis... I'm sorry!"

The question for you to consider is, "Would you do anything different or would your mental focus be directed any differently during the next six months than it has in the past six months?" One of the more memorable teaching moments of my life came in Auburn Hills, Michigan, when I asked seminar participants the same question after creating the exact same scenario. One gentleman in the training room of about fifty people, stood abruptly without notice and responded loudly at first, "You're _ right you would!" He then paused and solemnly announced to this group of mostly strangers, "that has just happened to me, and you better believe that you think about things differently, your focus changes to the really important things." You could have heard a pin drop. He went on to share with us how his daily concerns had shifted and how he had started paying more attention to "First Things First." I had a very responsive group when I asked to move them to take a moment and write a short list of the things that mattered most to them. You should do the same. Right now! Stop reading and write down three to six of your greatest values.

A few years ago, a San Francisco earthquake provided another spawning device to consider one's values. Interstate 880 had collapsed after the earthquake creating the sound of crushing cars by the falling of the upper level of concrete highway onto the lower. Five foot high vehicles were crushed into eighteen inch pancakes. In this instance, a civilian man heard the cry of a child several feet into the center of the eighty feet span. He realized in order to help, he must crawl into the eighteen inch crawl-space toward the crying child, understanding that an after shock was both imminent and probable. Crushed automobiles lost fuel and there was a strong smell of gasoline, hence a fiery explosion was also a high possibility. Risking his life, this man crawled in to save the child.

For what would you be willing to go into a dangerous thirty-inch crawl space? What do you value enough to risk your own life? What really matters to you? Take a minute and list a few of the truly important things in your life.

Considering crisis moments is one way to identify your values, because it helps you sense what matters. Another less threatening and effective way to clarify what matters most to you is to approach the task from a completely different mind-set. Remembering the truth that when our actions are congruent with our values, we experience a sense of inner peace, joy, or super satisfaction that helps us identify our values. Think back to a time in your life when you were the very happiest. Scan your mind for the great moments of your life, where you experienced true joy. In remembering and savoring those moments, you can extract your values. Your actions produced inner peace because you were paying attention to the value. What was the value being acted upon that produced those feelings?

Let's process this a little more deeply. Let me invite you to consider and reflect upon your past. Identify a time or times in your life when you felt really happy. Happiness is not really an adequate word to identify the feelings I am inviting you to recall. Others have stretched the word "happiness" to other expressions like "bliss," "inner peace," or joy. You may need to think about it for awhile, and it may not be easy. Your examination of the "great moments" in your life may give you some important clues to what your deepest values are.

You will likely discover several times in your life when you felt joy, inner peace, a certain happiness, or wellness. Maybe it was at a time when you didn't have financial worries. It is often found in times when people are very close emotionally, when spirit touches spirit, and each are edified or made stronger. Maybe it was when you were hunting, skiing down a mountain in perfect powder or resting on the bank of a stream at a moment of respite during a backpacking expedition. It could have been when you traveled into the unknown. I have personally found it in a grove of trees in upstate New York, in the Grand Canyon, even walking on a crowded street in Manhattan, and at the north shore of the Sea of Galilee. I find joy in my memories of sitting on a bench in Mexico City in a drenching rain smelling the diesel fumes of a passing bus. I also find clues in memories of sitting near the top of the Grand Teton in the mountains of Eastern Idaho and Western Wyoming or walking hand-in-hand with my spouse on a windy beach in

Oregon. As I scan more of the treasures of my past, I recall the special moments of yesteryear when our three-year-old ran down the hall, just ahead of the proverbial "boogie man," and bolted into our bedroom at three a.m. and jumped into bed next to me. She put her arms around my neck and cuddled next to me finding security and safety from the black of the night. The list continues; being with my business partner after we closed a deal, hugging my seventy-nine year old father, teaching a group of college students a principle I knew would make their lives better.

Once you have identified the moment, then probe deeper into WHY you felt special feelings of joy. As you discover the reason, write it down. You might get a piece of paper and try this approach:

Example 1:

Moment of time: In 19_, when living in _, employed by_.

Why was I happy then?: We weren't worried about money. We were being compensated enough that money wasn't a daily gnawing issue.

What is the Value?: Financial Wellness

Example 2:

Moment of time: 19_, reading an article in my high school newspaper which highlighted the best game I ever played.

Why was I happy then?: Realizing others were reading the same thing and would appreciate the contribution I made to our school pride.

Value(s): Recognition or maybe competence or achievement or teamwork.

Example 3:

Moment in Time: Sitting and talking with my friend

Why was I happy then?: We were not only laughing and enjoying each other, we were sharing personal feelings about living.

Values: Friendship, Spontaneous Introspection, Sharing.

NOTE: Once in a while a person will say to me, "I have thought and thought and I have a hard time identifying any period of my life where I felt really happy." If you find it hard to identify happy moments as a beginning point in isolating your values, first of all let me remind you that you're okay. If you think you would feel some peace in talking to a therapist, then make an appointment immediately with a qualified professional with whom you feel comfortable. However, you might first want to simply take a reverse approach to the quest of identifying your values. Take courage, then find three or four of the worst moments in your life—times when you considered life to be almost unbearable. Once you have those in mind, ask yourself, "Why was I miserable?" Follow that question by asking, "What was missing in my life that caused so much pain?" In our most miserable moments we can often identify our values by noting the INCONGRUENCE between those things we value and what was being done at the moment.

I personally have isolated two of my own values as I reviewed the darkest days of my life. My first recommendation is to look for the positive issues of your life. If, however, you find difficulty in successfully finding happy moments, let your brain go ahead and reverse the process.

Another way to clarify values is to first make a long list of values such as:

A satisfying and fulfilling marriage
Freedom to do what you want
A chance to direct the destinies of a nation
Love and admiration of friends
Travel
Self-confidence and a positive outlook on life
A happy family relationship
Being unusually attractive and recognized as being beautiful
A life free of illness
A library of the best books
A satisfying religious faith
Financial security
A world without prejudice
A chance to eliminate poverty from the world
International fame and popularity
An understanding of the true meaning of life
Success in a chosen profession
Adventure in life
Etc.

Now assume you have a thousand dollars and are at an auction where you are able to bid on and buy as many of those values as you want. All other buyers at the auction have exactly the same amount of money as you—one thousand dollars. You need to know which values you want to buy, remembering that if any in the buying group have a common value, the cost may be high. In fact you may only be able to purchase three, two, or perhaps only one value. What value would you be willing to lay your entire thousand dollars on? If someone else beat you on that value, which is your second choice, third choice, etc.?

Rescripting and Building Vision

Now that you have at least three or four values in your mind and have listed those things that matter most in your life, let's start the process. Notice on the following pages three examples of how others have given definition to their values.

Example A:

I am financially secure.

I make more money than I spend.

I save 10% of my income.

I have adequate life, health, and disability insurance to protect me in event of loss.

I budget my earnings to include meeting all of the needs of my family.

I share part of all I earn with others, to help those less fortunate.

Example B:

I am an excellent employee.

I understand what is expected of me.

I complete all that is expected of me and then find other ways which I can contribute to the success of my employer.

I assist in the team process.

Example C:

I am a good friend.

I make an effort to meet the needs of my friends.

I keep in contact with my best friends.

I make sincere and honest compliments to those I spend time with.

I smile at others and affirm their goodness.

What do you notice about the three examples? How are they written? What is their grammatical style? They are all written in the affirmative. In other words, they are written as if they have already happened or are consistently being acted upon today. Notice how they do not say "I want to ..." or "someday I hope to be able to ..." They state affirmatively "I am ... ," "I do ... ," and "I feel ..." Remember the Arts of Positive Self Talk and Positive Vision in Chapter 8, where we discussed the learnable skills pertaining to the Law of Expectation? As we first identify and then clarify our values, we are going to move them into self-talk scripting and vision building status. Remember, everything in our lives begins, continues, and ends with the way we talk to ourselves." Also remember that that which we play on the stage of our minds is a preview of a coming attraction. If these are true, (and they are), then we can use this process to change or enhance our actions toward more congruency with our values. We can live better and enjoy more inner peace and happiness because we are doing what matters. We do what matters more consistently because first we know what the value is, second, we have identified it in specific terms so we know what it looks like, and third, we have shaped it into positive self talk.

Do you remember from earlier reading, we learned that the subconscious mind cannot tell the difference between the imagined and the real? The mind will accept whatever you tell it. It is like a sponge which believes anything, even a lie. Since that is true, then we can tell it in specific terms what we "are" and give it a picture of the positive or affirmative and our actions will begin to more consistently line up with the instruction. Do you remember how the athletes of Russia and East Germany trained in the gymnasiums of their minds, through the process of autogenic conditioning? If you remember these things, then you will understand what we are trying to do with this critical exercise and component of creating your Creed Document.

Let's Try It

Take out a piece of paper. Bring one of the values you have previously identified, and write it down at the top of the paper. Then a line or two down, write this question: "What does it mean?" As you write affirmative or positive statements about this value continue to ask, "What does it mean?" or "What else does it mean?" Writing, asking and answering in this way does two important things. First, it drafts a new self-talk script and secondly, it takes a nebulous watercolor-like mental picture of your value and brings it into sharp focus. You can see what it means and you can read a script which identifies it in specifics.

We learned earlier that we will always act congruently with our values in crisis moments. In the non crisis moments of our lives, we don't always act in a manner congruent with our values. Why? Because we don't always know what they are. We may think we know, but often we don't, or they are so nebulous and out of focus, we can't see them in specific terms as we walk through daily life. Therefore, we do dumb things and feel badly. Our objective is to move us to the progressive side of the living continuum and to enjoy the inner peace and happiness we deserve in the non-crisis moments which dominate our daily lives.

Once we identify and give clarity to the "Things . Which Really Matter Most" in our lives by writing them down and creating a positive image of "what they mean" in specific terms, we can begin the process of internalizing them and making them a permanent part of our self talk and vision. Many great people have understood and harnessed this powerful process in their lives. Benjamin Franklin, for example, arrived at mid-life and found that the misery, failure, and poverty he had created for himself in the first half of his life needed change. Unless he started doing things differently, he knew he would continue to experience more of the same negative outcomes he had experienced to that point. He chose thirteen values to which he would dedicate the rest of his life. He determined that he would undertake a process where each week he would focus his attention and efforts on one of his thirteen values. He created a thirteen week rotation system covering each consecutive value. It changed his life. The rest of his story shows that this "transition," "transformation," "realignment," and "development" exercise changed his life to produce the powerful statesman, wealthy entrepreneur, and one known for his simple but profound wisdom.

I have studied many other great people who have done the same kind of exercise. I personally have identified seven major value areas for my life. Instead of a thirteen week cycle, I use a daily rotation system. Each day I rotate to one of my seven values. I read the affirmative statements, and ask myself how I am doing and what more I can do to be more congruent with that value TODAY. I have collected poems, inspiring thoughts, and pictures which typify or embody the value. I will spend a few minutes each rotation reviewing one or more of those enrichment items. While I am far from being 100% congruent everyday with my values, I am finding that I do more things rightly and experience the joy and inner peace more frequently than I have ever before. My new self talk script surfaces more often, and saves me from inappropriate non-congruent actions and finds me doing more things right. I am happier with each passing year.

For example, one of my values has to do with my family. That family value is divided into four subsets; I am a spouse, a father, a son, and a brother. Each are treated in my Creed and are written in the affirmative, positive, and answer the key question "what does it mean?" For instance, my Family Value as a Father is written as follows: "I am a Great Father." By using short succinct bullet statements I define what it means to me. "I love each of my eight children" is the first. Second, "My children are proud of me and want their friends to know that I am their Dad." Next bullet reads "I understand that the moments of highest positive impact in my children's lives come to me at the most inconvenient moments." There continues nine other statements which identify what it means to me to be a "Great Father."

Each seventh day in my life I review those statements, which takes them into my internal dialogue (self talk) script. I ask myself how I am doing and what more can I do to make those positive vision statements a reality. I believe that the most important thing that is happening is that I am affirming and reaffirming a new self talk script and visual image. I am preparing privately for public victories.

To illustrate, let me share one of my values with you, in the hopes that you will understand more completely how this process changes behavior. In 1988 our family decided to move from sunny Arizona to the Detroit Metropolitan area. Arizona was going through a major economic correction and houses were hard to sell. Prices of homes fell daily, it seemed. We felt it would be good to get our children settled into their new surroundings before school started in the fall, and the opening date was fast approaching. I was deeply concerned about selling our home. Our packed boxes and nearly all the household furniture items waited in the garage to be picked up by the moving company. The family room was bare with the exception of the sofa, a few floor pillows, and the TV.

One afternoon, a day or two before we actually left Arizona, I had been outside in the intense August heat. (It was about 117 degrees that day). I walked into the aforementioned family room where I noticed four of my children with about four friends each, as afternoon guests watching a video. Six or seven children were on the sofa and the rest on the floor, with eyes glued to the television set. They did not notice my entry into the room. But, I immediately saw a large silver stainless steel bowl which had been full of buttery popcorn. The bowl was tilted up and to one side; empty of its contents. The greasy popcorn was in little pile next to the bowl, apparently spilled unknowingly. I became very angry. My mind raced with "Don't these darn kids have any sense? Here we are having a hard time selling our home, and we now have a new major grease spot on the family room floor!" Oh, I must tell you, I was angry! I could feel a new heat sensation, different from the Arizona summer sun I felt a few minutes before. It was heat generated by my internal system. I was very mad at my children and their mindless friends. I marched into the room ready to turn off the TV and deliver a verbal lashing on the whole of them. Oh, was I angry! But split seconds before I started the speech I never delivered, a thought came to my mind—a thought I had read and internalized once each week for months, surfaced in its pure and exact form. "My children are proud of me and want their friends to know that I am their Dad." As that thought entered my mind, it caused me to pause long enough to think about what I was doing, what the real *issues* were, and what I should do next. "OK, David" I thought "it's the popcorn isn't it ... the popcorn creating a grease spot on the floor that *is* the real issue here. These kids are responsible and need to be taught but the real other issue is the relationship they will have with me next week, next year, and especially here in front of their friends." Still angry and emotionally "put-off" by their lack of awareness, I went to the pile of popcorn, set the large bowl upright and began to cleaning it up. The children, except one, were glued to the television and didn't even notice my entry into the room. She saw me walk into the room and then to the end of the sofa. This daughter, enthusiastically got up from the floor pillow, and put her hand out to assist a friend up who was beside her. From the corner of my eye, I saw them approaching but continuing to mutter under my breathe. "Dad" she said, and then paused when they arrived at the scene of the crime. "Oh, who spilled the popcorn?"

she continued. Still having a negative, almost abusive internal dialogue with myself about the stupidity of what had happened, I just looked up at her and issued what was surely an insincere smile. "Dad, this *is* Becky!" she blurted "she's my new friend. She just moved where the Jones used to live." Then she moved over a little closer to me, reached out and touched my elbow with her hand and with an enthusiastic grin on her face and a sparkle in her eye announced, "Becky, this is my Dad! He's awesome!"

I could tell that she was proud to tell her new friend who I was ...She went out of her way to introduce her. In that moment my self-talk dialogue changed from angry thoughts about mindless children to "Thank you, thank you! Thank goodness I didn't act like I felt." My new script saved me from myself. If my Family Value expressed in written terms and clear vision "my children are proud of me and want their friends to know that I am their Dad," is accurate, then my actions had better be congruent with that expression, or I will NOT be happy and have the inner peace I both desire and deserve.

Can you see how everything in our lives begin, continue, and end with the way we talk to ourselves? Can you see how the clarity of our visual images expressed in written terms are the "previews of coming attractions." Without the script and the positive vision flashing into my mind at precisely the critical moment, I would have come into the room that hot August afternoon and said things in front of my children's friends, which would have come back to haunt me. My relationship with some of the most important people in my life would have become tarnished. My outburst might have caused my children to look away, bury their heads in their pillows, get up and walk out of the room, or in essence say to their friends "we don't know who he is, but he's not anybody we want you to meet."

Of course after the friends had gone, we had a talk about buttery popcorn and greasy spots on the carpet. I wish I could report to you that our lives were changed forever ...no more spilled popcorn and no more misdirected actions on my part. I can report and attest that I am more often successful acting congruently with my values. Why? Because they are written in terms which are becoming a part of my internal dialogue or self talk. It *is* because I know what my values are—in some detail.

A Universal Principle and Process

Let's look at some examples outside of our personal arenas. First, look at the business community. Several years ago Tom Peters and Robert Waterman researched and wrote the business classic *In Search of Excellence*. In their work they sought to identify the excellent companies in America and look deeply into the characteristics that made them great. One of the hallmark discriminating attributes of successful companies in America is simply that they had identified their values and clearly expressed the actions congruent with those values. In other words, knowing what was valued, and acting out those values in specific ways, earned them a "blissful business life." This business bliss produces success, longevity, quality, effectiveness, and profitability.

Most will agree that the Ray Krock Story in building the internationally recognized and acclaimed name of "McDonald's," is one of the great business success stories of the century. If the McDonald's chain is great (and I believe they are) then it only follows that we ought to be able to look at any McDonald's Restaurant, their employees, their product, and in essence their ACTIONS and work backwards to identify their values. So what are they? You don't have to sit in the Corporate Board Meetings to know the answer to that question. Simply look at the Corporate Behavior and you can tell they have a strong sense of knowing who they are and "what their values mean in specific actions." So what are they?

Consistency, Cleanliness, Friendly, and Fast, to name a few. Whether you enjoy a Big Mac or not, if you eat one in London, Mexico City, or in Montana, you can always expect the same consistent taste, exactly! World over, you can go into a rest room at McDonald's, even where cleanliness is not the social norm, and you will find a clean rest room. You are always greeted with a smile and your order is processed within minutes.

Nations are operated by values. We call their Creed Document a "constitution." I am an American and pleased to be so. The founding fathers of this country got together and hammered-out the document which would become the guide for the way we live our social lives here in this country. We have amended or changed it on a few occasions "by the voice of the people," when we have felt it appropriate. As I scan back over the history of this nation, I am proud to be an American. But there have been eras or periods of time when the ACTIONS of the nation were not congruent with the basic values upon which we were built. In those moments of history, I am not proud. I am ashamed. In every case, my evaluation exhibits that our ACTIONS were not congruent with our values or our national Creed Document. There were times when people's feet were chopped off for their desire to be free—a basic tenant or value upon which this nation was built. There were glitches of time, times when we treated gender rights issues with undeniable and obvious prejudice. These were times when we fought and spilled the blood of far too many young Americans on foreign soil, without real cause or purpose. At times our actions as a nation towards Native Americans, African-Americans, many of our immigrants, early Mormon settlers, the Amish, and even the environment has been less than honorable. I am saddened as I consider what happened in this nation during those "glitches" when we were out of focus or off beam. Yes, when we have acted outside the parameters of our value system or national creed, we find moments of national shame.

The same is true in your life and mine. When our actions are not consistent with our values, our creed, or personal constitution, we find moments of regret and personal shame. It happens every time! Our frustrations with our own actions are heightened when we forget about who we are. Just as corporations not consistently acting in congruence with their company values, soon find their profitability and longevity jeopardized; we as individuals also find our personal "profitability" and capacity to perform sabotaged and reduced.

Summary

Remember our objective and purpose. Whether we are approaching or are in a transition in our life, it is a critical intersection when we must evaluate our values and create a powerful force of knowing who we are, what we value (in specific and identifiable terms), and programming ourselves to act accordingly through powerful self-talk and vision of positive outcomes. This exercise is one of the most important in the quest for change, realignment, and development. You will feel more positive movement in your personal life from this exercise than perhaps any other because it builds from your beliefs of WHO you are, into WHY you are and it gives positive definition to your life. Do it!

ASSIGNMENT

1. Make a list of your highest and most important values. You may want to use one of the methods listed previously in this chapter or you may use any other method which helps you to identify your values.

2. Process each one of them by first, expressing them in a positive affirmation. For example if the value is "health," then you would express it something like "I am healthy" or "Health is very important to me." Now take each value statement and ask yourself "So what does that mean?" What does it mean to be healthy? Now build several affirmation statements which describe what it means to be healthy.

3. Be sure each is in affirmative or positive form. Reread them and ask yourself "is this what it really means to me?" and "is there anything else I've left out which would give the value more clarity and understanding?"

4. As the weeks come and go, you may find you'll want to groom your first draft even more. Writing your values creates a process which will help crystallize them in your mind as well as bring them into focus with accurate perception.

Chapter Twelve

THE POWER OF GOALS

Knowing WHY you want something has to do with your values. Knowing WHAT you want and HOW you plan to achieve it is the basis of your goals and objectives. Beliefs are those opinions based on principles which you have accepted as truth. Your values are an extension of your beliefs but are the motivators of ACTION. Values are the fuel which gets things done in your life because they are the WHY or REASON for action. We are now ready to proceed to the next step, identifying the Goals (what you want) and Objectives (how you will go about getting what you want).

The Law of Growth

There is a law which states "All growth is outside the comfort zone." My life has been effected by a great poem which I found when I was a sophomore in high school. It was written on a wadded-up piece of paper which I discovered in the back seat of my car. I am sure it was discarded by one of my school friends when I gave them a ride home after school. But, because of the great impact it has had on my life, it could have been left there by an angel from heaven. I believe this poem has had as much practical influence on my life as anything.

Trees

The tree that never had to fight
For sun and sky and air and light,
But stood out on the open plain
And always got its share of rain,
Never became a forest king
But lived and died a scrubby thing.

The man who never had to toil to live,
Who never had to win his share
Of sun and sky and light and air,
Never became a manly man
But lived and died as he began.

Good timber does not grow-with ease
The stronger wind, the stronger trees
The further sky, the greater length
The more the storm, the more the strength.

By sun and cold, in rain and snow In
trees and men good timber grow
Where thickest lies the forest growth
We find the patriarchs of both.

And they hold council with the stars
Whose broken branches show the scars
Of many winds and much of strife
This is the COMMON LAW OF LIFE.

Author Unknown

The "common law of life" is simply that "Growth comes to us when we are stretching and anxiously engaged in doing good things outside the comfort zone." Weight lifters gain more strength and muscle power by always adding a little more weight or by increasing the number of repetitions. The rose bush produces more beautiful flowers when it's trimmed, cut back, and pruned. All growth is stimulated outside of the comfort zone. Setting and achieving goals is the process of always pushing the outer edge of the comfort zone with the understanding that we will become a better and better person.

The Great Dilemma of 3% versus 97%

In each of the many studies on Goal Setting and its process, successful people in all arenas of life are goal setters. People do not fall into success long term. Sure, some may win the lottery, receive an inheritance, or fall into some luck and experience a "flash" of financial success. But if they are not goal setters, they will soon be back to whatever level of financial wellness they were in before their fortune injected a season of bliss. Goal setting is a private victory which is a key to winning public victories. The dilemma in my mind is why—with so much evidence that GOAL SETTING is paramount to successful living, and in a nation which is as progressive as the United States, do we have so little, if any, formal instruction on the subject in our school systems? After over eighteen years of formal education with four degrees and numerous hours of study, I cannot identify one time in my school life where I was taught the value of goals, how to achieve them, or any information collected from the studies about them. The closest I have come in the public school setting to any informal instruction on goal setting was in my athletic life from coaches who wanted to produce winning teams. Most of those experiences were so fraught with yelling, negative vision, and criticism that any real good from those experiences was diminished. I have spent over 20,000 hours in class time as a student and have never received any instruction about how to understand the value of and importance of identifying goals, setting objectives, and proceeding to make my life more meaningful. I want to make it clear that I appreciate my teachers and the many good things they taught me outside the textbook or examination questions. However, the question I pose is simply whether or not developing the skills of setting goals, visualizing results, and meeting a level of achievement in our life's endeavors merits some instruction in the formal curriculum of our country's classrooms?

To me, the dilemma thickens! You may have heard of an interesting study completed several years ago by a student at Yale University. I have heard it cited many times and am making an effort to document it. In my efforts to do so I believe the following to be the most reliable information on the study. In 1953, a student prepared a thesis on the issue and importance of setting goals. In the body of the thesis the student completed a rather significant study and statistical review which revealed that only 3% of the graduating class at Yale that year considered, evaluated, set, and ultimately wrote down their goals. It was suggested that the process of writing down the goals is an important facet of goal setting. Several other studies reveal that only 3 to 5% of adults in America, the Land of the Free, feel excited enough about their ambitions that they will write them down and review them often. That is a dilemma to me! Perhaps the most interesting dimension of the aforementioned Yale study is in what happened twenty years later in 1973. A graduate student from another prestigious university conducted a similar study and found similar results. However, as a part of the dissertational theme, this student used the Yale study of two decades earlier as a foundation for her premise that writing goals down on paper makes a difference in the outcomes or results. She postulated that the process of writing goals down was a chief exercise ingredient in achievement of those goals. She decided that she would go back and track down the graduating class twenty years earlier at Yale. The student did a remarkable job of locating and interviewing each alumni. While a few were deceased, the majority were contacted and willingly participated in the study. It is difficult to define success, let alone evaluate it, therefore it was determined that the only real statistical merit of success that could be evaluated was the financial dimension of the lives of those Yale alumni. Her findings were so unusual that the doctoral committee questioned its validity, based on inconclusive data. The committee consensus was that there must be other variables contributing to her findings. At the insistence of the committee she went back and tried to determine if there were financial inheritance variables, some stroke of unplanned fortune, or similar causes which would explain her findings. She discovered none. Her study revealed that the 3% who had developed the habit of writing their goals down had more financial net worth than the 97% combined. I think this is one of the best longitudinal studies. I will not suggest to you that if you will write your goals down on paper, you are insured extraordinary financial success. However, the implications of the two studies give us something to think about. Maybe there is something which happens in the process of writing down goals and reviewing them often which peaks our achievement mechanism and turns dreams into reality. Maybe we should at least ask ourselves if we could increase our productivity and improve our lives twenty five percent by setting goals and writing them down then reviewing them often, would we do it? What if we could improve the outcomes of our lives by only ten percent with this habit? Would it be worth it to invest the few minutes each day that would be required? I think so!

Now whether or not the story and study of the 3% and 97% is an urban legend or even as outright hoax, I have polled my students, seminar participants, and friends many times to determine how many of them are in a habit or practice of writing down their goals on paper. It is a dilemma to me how over and over again, I get the same results in these informal surveys. Usually three to five out of every 100 admit to the practice. Why those statistical numbers? Why do the numbers not change in academia, professional circles, or athletic playing field? Why 3%? Furthermore, when we look at a hundred people in any arena of life, why it is that a corresponding statistic, 3%, are in the winner's circle in their life or endeavor? Why is it that those 3% who are successful are also goal setters who write down, review, rethink, revise, and rewrite their goals? It's worth paying attention to.

If the practice of writing down and reviewing goals is a critical component of winning the private victories, I want to do what I can to raise that figure from three percent, if only in the circles I work in. If I could convince you to embrace this new private victory principle in your life (along with another ten percent of those who read this book) thousands of lives could be made better. Maybe in time we could move the percentage up, and in the wake of doing so we would create more fulfilled and happy lives. Will you help me in my crusade?

I invite you to make a personal commitment to do it now. If not now, then within the next ten days of your life. Make an appointment with yourself! Sit and write down your goals! It will be an energizing process which will create a new momentum in your life.

Enemies of the Process

It is always good to evaluate the obstacles in any effort to succeed, to the end that we will be more equipped to win the battle. We are responsible for our success or failure. Let's take a look at verifiable obstacles which get in the way of goal setting. Two of the more obvious obstacles are:

1. **Lack of Understanding**

    We don't fully understand the importance of goal setting or the process of writing them down. While we are responsible for our lives, chances are good that if you are not a goal setter or not in the practice of crystallizing your goals in writing, you are not entirely at fault. We know that goal setting parents usually produce goal setting children. Writing and setting goals is not a genetic concern. But what we talk about when we sit at the dinner table and whether or not our parents shared their goals with us by encouraging us to be dreamers, is a family concern. Instilling the dreaming attitude and bringing dreamer instincts to our lives is important. Whether or not your parents were goal setters and instilled the same in you, it is a critical obstacle to understand that it is important. Do you?

2. **Fear**

    Fear is a debilitating emotion. I believe it is the culprit in preventing the masses from becoming more of what they could be through the goal setting processes. First, we all fear failure. We don't like to fail. It is painful to fall short of desired outcomes, unless we change the

---

principle on our Belief Window. If we can accept that failure is fertilizer and an important part of success, then perhaps we are on our way. If we don't, then we fear the personal humiliation which can come to each of us when we fail. We don't write our goals down and become goal setting because we fear we will fail. So it's easier to just quietly proceed in the arms of the comfort zone. We don't try. We fail to strive and by failing to strive we simply shift slowly, but surely backward by the power of entropy. Fear of failure is an obstacle.

Second, Fear of Rejection pervades the mind of most non-goal setters. If I announce my goals to others, they may reject me. They may laugh and say, "oh sure, so you think you can achieve that?" Have you ever been very excited about a possibility, some lofty thought of :cess, and then when you told a friend or loved one, they gave eighteen reasons why you shouldn't, or couldn't, or would not able to achieve the realization of it? Those people are the "wishers" who march with the masses of the 97%, wishing things were different, consigning themselves to the comfort zone. They will never make it to the top of any mountain and will spend their idle days telling everyone else all the reasons why it can't be done. Understanding this fear and how ridiculous it is will assist us in conquering it.

Third, is the fear of success. Yes, you read it right, "fear of success." Isn't it strange that some people get into a mind set of fearing success. They have what Denis Waitley calls "permanent potential." They have all of the tools for success: they look great, they are motivated, they even set some goals, but right at the moment when they are about to score, they self-destruct. They find a way to fall short of the finish line. Why? They fear that if they succeed, then more will be expected of them, new challenges will be given, and more responsibility to succeed will be publicly expected. Their self-esteem teeters to the point that they will always fall back into the pool of failure rather than forward into the limelight of success where they will be expected to stay and perform again and again. It's too hard and energy-consuming as they consider the need to continue to produce more. Hence, they have "permanent potential," almost succeeding and then failing over and over again. They fear success.

We have not unveiled anything new. The obstacles can be many but usually fall into one or more of the areas above. The important thing is to understand that Goals make up an invisible force which is real! They are a real pull toward your future. People with written goal centered lives are drawn to the future with excitement, enjoyment, and anticipation for a better life in the future. They find opportunities to improve, transform themselves or their circumstances, and change. However, the obstacles are those things which get in the way of improvement, then invisible power is reversed to an energy push, instead of pull. The masses of humanity are being pushed around, managed by popular opinion, fads, and follow the road of least resistance. Instead of being drawn to a better life, they are shoved, forced, and blown about by every wind of public opinion. Goal writers and reviewers are fueled by their values and drawn toward the future with purpose and excitement.

How to Design Your Goals

Designing a life and a future is lacing your life with wonderful anticipation vs. living it with apprehension. There are some things that will help us get started and get our creative juices flowing. First of all, it is important to understand a concept which I call "A Goaling" and "Z Goaling." "A Goaling" is to insure that your important life goals spring directly out of your values. In other words, you have already created the basis for your "A Goaling" by identifying and processing your values in the previous chapter. You simply take each one of your values and the accompanying statements of what they mean, and ask yourself "WHAT DO I WANT TO ACHIEVE IN THIS VALUE AREA?" and "HOW WILL I GO ABOUT DOING IT?"

For example, if I have the value of Health, I will have written scripting statements to improve my self-talk and give my value specific definition like "I get sufficient sleep but not more than is needful." Another, "I weigh consistently between 203 and 210 pounds." Or another, "I exercise no less than once every 48 hours." As I look at my value of health and what the value means expressed in scripting and visual statements I ask myself, "WHAT SPECIFIC GOAL WOULD I LIKE TO ACHIEVE IN THIS AREA?"

Let's assume that I take the idea that "I exercise no less than once every 48 hours of my life." From that statement, I can extract and process a GOAL, a "What" I want and a list of "HOW" to accomplish it. My Goal might be to engage in cardiovascular activity three to four days each week. What questions naturally follow? What aerobic exercise will I do? Which exercise do I enjoy the most? Which cardiovascular exercise is the best to accomplish

---

my goal? 'What time of the day will I do it? Will I do it alone or will I get someone to join me to increase the commitment level? Will I do only one specific exercise or can I give my program variety by combining two or three activities? Is there reading material or published research on this subject which will enhance my understanding on this subject? The list of questions goes on.

From the answers to these questions we begin to build our "HOW" list. Our "how" list then becomes the basis for the things we do each day. They are the action items that move us to accomplishing the goal itself. In other words, as we answer the important questions about the GOAL (What we want), we create a "punch list" of things to do, which automatically answers the question "HOW will I do it?"

My list might look like:

> Go to bookstore and choose a book on "aerobic exercise"
>
> Read no less than two chapters each day
>
> Get an appointment with Dr. Heiner for a physical check-up
>
> Get opinion from Dr. Heiner re: benchmark sub-goals
>
> Talk to Tom and Paula to see if they want to join me
>
> Pick up running shoe catalog at Gart Bros. Sporting Goods
>
> Talk to Dr. Barton for recommendations for shoes
>
> Select and order shoes
>
> Identify a reward for each bench mark success
>
> Begin program on 3-3-9_
>
> Monitor progress toward subgoals on 4-12-9_

Each day as we invest our 1% or 14.4 minutes (living the Law of 1%), we review the list and pull in an appropriate "action" item to include in the "things to do today." Hence, day by day we are moving closer to the GOAL and at the same time we are living congruently with our VALUES, because we are doing something to keep the "health plate" spinning. We are paying attention to something we have identified as important. The greatest by-product of the action is the internal satisfaction of knowing we are being pulled toward doing things that will make us successful.

"A Goaling" is a function of looking at each of our values and identifying one or more goals within that value which we want to work toward. Then building a list of specific tasks or action items to accomplish those goals. Can you see why WRITING them down on paper and tracking each item is critical? You cannot over emphasize the importance of WRITING down your goals and creating the punch list of things to do.

We will talk about "Z Goaling" later but let's look at some other important Keys to effective goal development.

Keys to Effective Goal Development

Key 1: Understand the Comfort Zone

All growth, ALL GROWTH, is outside our comfort zone. Growth, change, transformation is in doing things differently than we have been doing up to this point. To change results, we must change actions. Remember the Chinese definition for "insanity" which applies here: Insanity is "doing the same thing, in exactly the same way, and expecting different results." We must get out of our comfort zone if we are going to improve.

We are not talking about being a "reckless risk taker" or having what someone calls the "Lottery Syndrome"—taking chances and living on the edge. We are talking about and inviting ourselves to check and see if we have the "Security Syndrome." Always living in the security of the proverbial comfort zone will insure sameness, stagnation, and ultimately the "Potted-plant Syndrome" (root-bound atrophy). All growth, stimulation, and positive change is outside the comfort zone.

Key 2: Sincere Desire

Ya-got-ta-wanna! We must have a desire to change and become more than what we have been to date. I once heard a poem by an unknown author which states:

If you want a thing bad enough to go out and fight for it
    Work day and night for it,
    Give up your time and your peace and your sleep for it
If only the desire of it makes you mad enough to never tire of it,
    Makes you hold all things tawdry and cheap for it,

Life seems all empty and useless without it,
    And all that you scheme and dream *is* about it,
If gladly you'll sweat for it, fret for it, plan for it
    Lose all your terror of devils and men for it,
If you'll simply go after the thing that you want,
    With all your capacity, strength, and sagacity,
    Faith, hope, and confidence, stern pertinacity,
If neither cold, poverty, famish nor gaunt,
    Nor sickness, nor pain of body or brain,
    Can keep you away from the thing that you want,
If dogged and grim, you beseech and beset
    You'll get it. You'll get it.

Author Unknown

You simply have to want WHAT you want. Desire is a fundamental ingredient which must exist or we will not achieve anything very meaningful. Ya-got-ta-wanna!

Key 3: **Understand the Enjoyment Factor**

Enjoyment is critical to long term successful goal attainment. There is something in the chemistry of billions of cells in the human body which know when you are having fun and enjoying what you do. The enjoyment emotions we experience seem to set in motion biochemical changes in our body and brain which generate peak performance. Enjoyment fosters positive emotions which make us faster, smarter, calmer, more energetic, and better at solving problems. Enjoyment draws upon intrinsic or internal wellsprings instead of extrinsic or external prodding, hence our performance flows from within. Enjoyment produces a powerful emotional flow sometimes called passion. When we act out of enjoyment the biochemistry of our emotions give us internal injections in just the right doses of norepinephrine, serotonin, endorphins, and other natural hormones which help us perform at peak levels.

While I don't pretend to know a lot about how all of these things work together, I am sure that we perform differently when we ENJOY what we do. You might want to investigate the merits of a wonderful best selling book by James Loehr and Peter McLaughlin entitled *Mentally Tough*. You will likely find it very interesting and enlightening. Further,

Norman Cousins, an internationally acclaimed author, medical doctor, and professor at the UCLA School of Medicine expounds on the enjoyment factor in his books. I recommend *Head First: The Biology of Hope* and *The Anatomy of an Illness*.

Consider that your goals should always be centered in WHAT you ENJOY. People in transition, especially, need to look deep within themselves and ask "What do I really enjoy? Where do I find my greatest enjoyment?" We not only perform at peak levels when we enjoy what we are doing, we find the preceding key—desire—natural.

I lived in Michigan for a chapter of my professional life. I frequently traveled north from Detroit on the interstate to do seminar work in Midland and Saginaw. I became intrigued with an unusual sight just off the interstate near Frankenmuth, Michigan. It was a year round Christmas Store. Investigation blessed my life with a wonderful story. Years ago a young man by the name of Wally Bronner was going to college to be a chemist. He thought that a Ph.D. in chemistry was a worthy goal. He had a hobby of painting signs and creating window displays for department stores. One day he received some great advice from a friend and mentor who said to him "Wally, if you want to have a successful career, find something you'd love to do 24 hours a day." Wally loved painting signs and creating window displays. His goal to become a chemist was fueled by public opinion and what others felt would create many career options and prestige. Chemistry was work. sign painting and window displays, though just a hobby, was pure enjoyment and an emotional outlet for Wally. You guessed right! Wally scrapped the potential and prestige of a Ph.D. in chemistry to follow his bliss—his enjoyment. His goal was to serve people by making signs and window displays. His enjoyment produced peak performance and soon businesses around the area were seeking his expertise. It wasn't long before his abilities were sought from around the state, then the entire country. His specialty was Christmas displays for commercial users. Soon came requests from private users. They wanted his displays for home use. Wally and his wife sat down and decided together that their enjoyment would be heightened even more if they could build a Christmas Store—not just for Frankenmuth, the state of Michigan, or the United States, but for the whole world. They built their first Christmas Store in 1954. Ten years later they had expanded to nine buildings, and they were still out of space. People were coming from around the world to Bronner's

Christmas Store in Frankenmuth, Michigan. Finally they bought forty-five acres and now have the largest, most profitable, and most amazing year round Christmas Store in the world. The Bronners followed their enjoyment.

What do you enjoy? Set your goals around your greatest enjoyments. When you do, you'll maximize the probability of great success. Your capacities are increased biologically, physiologically, and mentally when you enjoy what you do. Books are full of examples of success stories that come from the enjoyment factor.

Key 4: **Dream the Believable**

Successful goal setters are dreamers. Somehow, after we get older and wiser, we stop dreaming. I used to think that maybe there was something societal or cultural about the death of dreaming in America. I believe everything that is good in this country *is* built on dreams. I am now beginning to change my feelings of a few years ago when I thought that America had stopped dreaming. I am beginning to change my mind. I now postulate that "dream drought" may be more of a longitudinal or age phenomenon than a geographical one. I am beginning to think that maybe our dreams die sixty or seventy years before our bodies do.

I have conclusive firsthand evidence as I have watched my own children grow, that children before the age of 11 have unbelievable capacity to imagine and dream. I have watched them dream and pretend dress up, making a grocery store of my study, a luxury hotel of our family room, and Super Bowl XXX out of my backyard lawn. They dream and they scheme. They find the future in every moment. Then we adults start to "help" them grow up and get ready for real life. We inject their beautiful capacity to dream with "grow up and understand .that real life is hard." "Real-lifers" are usually the "Ghosts of Past Dreamers" who come back to haunt those who imagine the fanciful visions of how things can be. "Real-lifers" claim that anyone who mentally conceives of utopian shangri-las is prone to deceptive hallucinations or pipe dreams. I acknowledge that we must pass from the whimsical fairyland of childhood dreams to the realities of living. However, as we pass through that hellacious portal of adolescence where most everything that matters *is* shelved by the dictates of the peer group, dreaming begins to die. I submit that young people who break the connection with their dreams to follow the pack are the first to bury them. They are the first to look for the destructive substitutes of drugs, alcohol, and relationships. Those who hang on to their dreams a little longer often escape the aforementioned, but join the -masses in submitting to the Grim Reaper in becoming more logical, more adult-like, and more realistic in their approach to life. They entomb their dreams of really becoming "somebody" and settle on jumping through societal and cultural hoops, becoming adults.

Perhaps I'm wrong on how it all happens or even when it happens, but I am right that it does happen. The masses stop dreaming. When we stop dreaming we slide into the dining hall of commonness where we feed on the daily news of "federal trade deficits," "the stock market," "lost morality," "crime," "sliding employment," "the deterioration of the ozone," "extinction of the spotted owl," "possibility of nuclear holocaust," and "the world is going to hellisms." While we do have enormous challenges to face on our planet, it is in DREAMING that we will find the solutions.

Be a kid again! Sit back and dream! People in transition almost always need to rekindle their capacity to dream. I've always thought that the seed of hope is dreaming. What do you hope for? Can you see it? Can you believe it? Be careful to stay out of the discount business where you immediately begin to discount or whittle your dreams down to the common. Dream!

Napoleon Hill, a great dreamer and student of success, has said, "Whatever the mind can conceive and believe, it can achieve." Dream, conceive, and believe. As you do, goals will become more lofty and just far enough outside the comfort zone that you will develop the progression habit. Be sure to have a pad of paper with you and something to write with. Write, doodle, and crystalize your dreams to the written word.

Key 5: **Write it Down**

We have already spoken of the value of writing down our goals. This is likely one of the most important things you will ever do in the goal setting process. It has to get from the head and the heart to a piece of paper where you can look at it, refine it, and ultimately review it often. Besides expressing your goal in written sentences and terms, it is important that you make it as specific as possible. How big? What size?

What color? When? How much? Find a picture or doodle and make your own. Get out your calculator and work through several variations if there are monetary, time, or quantitative implications.

Key 6: **Focus, Focus, Focus, on the Benefit**

Almost everyone has the propensity to focus their attention on the results or outcomes. The benefit is usually an outgrowth of the REASON or the WHY which is the VALUE. If we can keep a focus on the BENEFITS of doing what we are doing, we will find the power to reach the goals. Instead of focusing on attaining a goal of getting a college degree, direct your attention to the benefit of having one. Perhaps it will be all of that knowledge you will acquire, or maybe it will be the recognition you will receive from loved ones or future employers. The benefit for you could be in giving of your knowledge to someone else. Do you understand? Focus on the benefits of a college degree, not on the piece of paper called the diploma or the milestone of the degree itself. There is a difference and you will find it. Focus on the benefits.

Personally, I have had a goal to be able to dunk or jam the basketball (that means go high enough on a ten foot rim to be able to put the ball down through the hoop vs. shoot it up to the rim and have it fall through the hoop). The result is to attain and retain the capacity to do that. The benefit has more to do with the feeling of being able to do something most other people in the late 40s cannot, or the kind of endorphins high in being able to do it. The benefits are far more important and energizing than the results or just arriving at some acquisition or attainment.

Key 7: **Where are you now?**

If we are standing in front of a Marriott Hotel in some city and intend to go to the airport and fly to Minneapolis, Minnesota, it would be an excellent thing for us to know which Marriott Hotel we are standing in front of and in what city. Our plans to get to Minneapolis pivot entirely on where we are right now. How we get to the airport is a function of where we are in relationship to it. How much it will cost in time and money to get to Minneapolis depends on of whether we are in London, Sydney, Orlando, Seattle, or Acapulco.

Define in specific terms where you are, in relation to where your written goals will take you. **Be** specific and again, WRITE it all down.

We tend to live in the "someday I'll" world. Someday I want to travel to Switzerland. Someday I want to own two snowmobiles. Someday I will write a book. Someday I want to get my degree. Someday I'll find the happiness I'm now searching for. The somedays rarely ever come nor do we catch up with them. They are illusive and intangible. The key is in giving our dreams a deadline.

One of the great AHA's that I had early in my married life was shortly after we finished college and received employment in the Phoenix area. We, like many of our friends, lived in apartments or rentals. I recall that frequently we would talk about "someday" moving into a neighborhood and buying a home. Most of the time we would hear ourselves, young couples with one child, saying things like, "when we get some money saved up for a down payment, then we'll buy a home," or "someday when we get our student loans paid off, then we'll get serious about looking for a home in our price range." One of the young couples came back from riding into the growing suburbs of the east valley. After looking at model homes in modest neighborhoods they said, "everything is too expensive, I can't see how we'll ever be able to afford a home, but maybe someday."

An older and wiser friend took me aside and said one day, "David, if you want to buy a home, just decide when you want to buy it ... set a date!" I went out to a model home or two, got floor plans and prices, got out my calculator and began to dream a little. I set a date two or three years out. Once I set the date, an interesting thing happened. The realtor had told me that I needed to have $2,000 for a down payment and another $500 for closing costs. That doesn't seem like anything now but in the early 70s for a young couple paying back student loans, buying a car, and just living, $2,500 was a chunk of change. However, when I wrote down a date or a self imposed deadline an interesting series of questions automatically popped up to be answered. Questions like "How much do I need to save each month between now and then? Are there other ways I can generate income? What about sweat equity with the builder, can I do my own painting, installing light fixtures, or landscaping?" As those questions surfaced and were answered, the deadline or date was moved closer. Then my mind seemed to go on autoscan, and I began to find other creative ways to generate solutions which again moved the date for our first home acquisition even closer. Instead of waiting for "three or four years" to get the down payment and qualify for a new home like the friendship committee (our friends) had defined and accepted, I concluded after my private "date setting and goaling" session, that we could do it in one year! Then I had one of the most important AHA's in my goal-setting life ... I didn't need $2,500 dollars! That's not what I needed at all. What I needed was $6.94 a day. I was almost spending that every day for lunch. Now my mind again reeled ... where could we save $6.94 a day for one year? I studied our budget, I considered secondary income sources, and finally concluded that we could pull it off in nine months. In nine months we could be living in our first home! I was so excited. I told my wife. She gave me one of those "you and Polyanna" looks as if to say "Davy," (she's the only one who has permission to call me by that name) "you know we can't ... we have student loans, car payments, and we're hoping to have a second child within a year. Get real!" After several hours of grueling teaching, I convinced her it could be done. We were so excited we told our friends. They smiled and kind of looked at us like we were complete idiots, and then said "that's great." I have no doubt that we were the subjects of discussion when we left ... something like "I hope Dave and Deena aren't setting themselves up for disappointment."

Well, the rest is history! We moved into our first new home within eight months. It all started by getting it out of our heads onto a piece of paper and generating the questions which would make it all a reality.

Key 9: **Identify the Obstacles**

After we have identified WHAT we want and HOW we will proceed, it is always worthwhile to ask ourselves to honestly assess the obstacles in our way. Where are the saboteurs that can, if given ground, defeat us in our quest of our goal?

Obstacles may appear much larger and loom far more ominously than they really are until we write them down. Somehow the writing down of the obstacle is the first step in dismantling it and making it impotent. Some people call this destructive disease which weakens our capacity to perform, the PLM Syndrome (Poor Little Me Syndrome). It is the fretting about life's obstacles with an attitude that "Poor Little Me" has so much to do and so little time that I just can't get it done! It is the feeling that we can't score a victory by reaching some goal because there are just too many things getting in the way. Personally I call this the MS (Mind-

Swarm) Syndrome. Somehow, unless I get the goal down on a piece of paper and look at it, my mind swarms with obstacles and reasons why I'm overwhelmed and can't get certain things accomplished, because there's just too much to keep me from it. The Mind Swarm Syndrome double and triple counts each obstacle until the mind accepts the false notion that "there are too many obstacles" I must accept. I expect to fall short on this goal.

Once my son, who was serving as the class president in his large high school and was active in several other endeavors, came in and sat down at the kitchen table. His shoulders were slumped and his attitude was dragging on the floor. He had the physical and emotional symptoms of MS Syndrome. "Dad," he said "I am so busy. My academic work is down. I am in charge of the Prom. I am working part-time. I am so overwhelmed, I feel like I am failing in everything!" Sure enough, he did have chronic MS Syndrome. I listened for several minutes as he re-counted the numerous reasons why he was on his way to "failure" in every dimension of his life. "Wow, sounds like you're pretty busy, stressed, and need something to give you a break," I said as I thought to prepare myself to answer his despondence. The Law of Opportunity reminds us that "life produces more to do than time to do it" and that sometimes we attempt to spin too many plates and maybe we can let some of those with less priority drop to the floor. We might have mistaken the issue for too many plates but I personally felt it was MS. I said, "Aaron, grab a piece of paper and let's write this stuff down." After about one minute we had identified the sum total of the OBSTACLES which were getting in his way. At first he couldn't believe it! As we looked at his three legitimate obstacles, he kept saying "Man, I know I'm forgetting something ... what is it? I know there are more things I am dealing with than this!" No, there wasn't anything else. The Mind Swarm Syndrome had double and triple counted his three obstacles, until he felt overwhelmed and unable to deal with the problems. Have you ever felt the same? Get a piece of paper and write down your obstacles. Identify them. This will insure you don't have MS Syndrome and will allow you to dismantle the problem one obstacle at a time. You'll find there are a lot less obstacles than you originally thought.

Key 10: **Who, What, Where do I need to go to for help?**

This key is "mentorship" in action. Who can help me understand the road to my goal? What knowledge should I get to insure my success? Where can I go for more help and insight into the anatomy of the process of achieving a certain goal. Find people, experiences, and everything you can about the goal before your begin. It will save you a lot of unnecessary back tracking and frustration in route to your goal achievement.

Key 11: Embrace the Law of Service as a guiding force in your goal

Any lasting or meaningful goal comes from serving others. Think about and write down "how reaching your goal" will make this world a better place. Another way of approaching it is to ask "What will I give to others as I am reaching my goal?" We live in a world which teaches us to ask "What's in it for me?" or "What will I get for the service I give?" The primary and extremely important question should be "WHAT CAN I GIVE?" The rest all flows naturally. Stay focused on the Law of Service. Ask and answer the question "What will I give?" over and over again.

Key 12: Faith

One definition of Faith is "the hope for things which are not seen, which are true." It is the quiet persistent hope that is an evidence of our faith that we can set, strive for, and ultimately attain a goal. Have the faith that you will realize the goals you set for yourself. Know that you can achieve and realize them. You'll get it!

"A Goals" come from your values. They are the things which you are striving for. What are your goals? What are the things you would want if you knew you could not fail? What is your great, value driven "WHAT?" Write it down!

"Z Goaling"

While the "A goals" are the really important value driven achievements in your life, "Z goals" are those extra "icing on the cake" kinds of things which make life interesting and sweet. If they don't happen, it's okay. They are seldom important in making your actions and values congruent. They are just the things which sweeten life. Sit down with a blank piece of paper. Perhaps you will want to listen to your favorite instrumental music. For ten or fifteen minutes just write down some things you'd like to experience but which are not seated necessarily in your values and are not really important in terms of achievement. You'll be creating a list of "icing on the cake" kinds of things you'd like to do. Examples from other peoples' "Z Goals" list are:

Ride in a hot air balloon

Bungee jump

Ride the whitewater of the Snake River

Paint a picture

Eat dinner with royalty (king, queen, prince, etc.)

Run in a marathon

Be an "extra" in a movie

Skydive

Restore a classic car

Participate in a tribal ceremony or dance

Find a buried treasure

Ride in a fighter jet

Author a book

See a crocodile in the wild

Swing through the trees on a vine

Your list can include anything you'd like to do which would make life a little more interesting and broaden your perspective. Remember, they are not intended to be the kinds of things which are critical to meeting and living by your values. Some people have reported that this list is best stimulated by looking at *National Geographic*, or *Life* Magazine, or the Discovery Channel on TV. Others enjoy quiet music and closing their eyes and just asking "What if ..." or "It would be really neat if I could ..." "Z goals" are just fun things to do and some of them may seem unusual or even impossible. Write them down!

Acres of Diamonds

There is a story told of an African farmer who wanted to search for diamonds and make his fortune. His passion became so great that he sold his farm and used the proceeds to finance his search. After a few years his money was depleted and soon he was penniless! He died a poverty stricken man. The irony of the situation comes in what followed a few years later. The person who bought his farm was inspecting his property one day and discovered a large rough stone in a stream bed. He took it to a gemologist and they discovered that the stone was a diamond "in the rough" but that it was one of the largest diamonds ever discovered. Inspection of the property near the stream bed yielded a phenomenal result. The diamond was one of many. In fact, right there on the farm, one of the richest diamond mines was discovered and mined. The new land owner became wealthy overnight. The original farmer had sold his farm to search for the precious stone, while all along, his fortune was on the very spot he gave up. Sometimes in setting goals we speculate and dream of "making it" in greener pastures. The truth is that most of the time your acres of diamonds will be found right where you are. Many get caught up thinking "success and happiness" is somewhere out there, while all along it is right where you are!

Write It Down!

Early in this chapter we postulated that the more committed you are to writing your goals down and reviewing them often the more you will be able to do. Author W. H. Murray writes:

> The moment one definitely commits oneself, then Providence moves too. All sorts of things occur to help, that would never otherwise have occurred. A stream of events issues from the decision, raising unforeseen incidents and meetings and material assistance, which no man could have dreamt would have come his way. I have learned a deep respect for one of Goethe's couplets: "What you can do, or dream you can, begin it. Boldness has genius, power, and magic in it."

Happy Goaling!

ASSIGNMENT

1. Review each of the values identified in the previous assignment in building your Creed Document (Part 4). In each value area, you will be able to find specific things you'd like to accomplish. Remember, "Values" are the WHY'S of your life. They are your REASONS or PURPOSE. Goals, on the other hand, are WHAT you want to achieve and Objectives are HOW you intend to get the WHAT (Goals) you want. Identify one or more goals for each of your VALUES.

2. Now create a listing of all the things or tasks you must complete in order to achieve, acquire, or complete the goal you wish to strive for.

    This part of your Creed Document will be the basis for your "daily task list." You will find that as you review it daily and pay attention to the things which must get done in order for you to achieve your goals, you will DO IT!

3. Make a list of "Z goals." Dream. What would make your life more exciting and interesting?

Chapter Thirteen

LIFE'S GREAT ENERGIZERS

L ike a proper balance of vitamins, minerals, protein, and carbohydrates give energy and increase our capacity to live dynamically, there are certain intakes into our behavioral mechanism which energize and propel us toward more meaning and success in our lives. We would do well to understand that these are often forgotten or misunderstood elements which ultimately will have great impact upon our capacities to live with excellence. While they are attitudinally influenced, they can become habits which make life unbelievably great.

The Law of Gratitude

The Law of Gratitude simply is that living with an "attitude of gratitude" enhances every outcome of the "Human Experience." Have you ever known someone who lives life angry at the weather, at bad service in every restaurant they enter, has a long list of pet-peeves which gives them license to be a critic of everything and everyone? Do you like that kind of person? Do they inspire you? Are you motivated by their example to strive for greater levels of excellence in your own life? Do you enjoy being around them?

In contrast, do you know someone who enjoys life? Someone who is a pleasure to be around, who positively stimulates you to do better and be more? Do they celebrate diversity instead of condemning anyone who doesn't think like they do? Likely, they are tolerant. They may be demanding, but always in a spirit of kindness, without hypocrisy, and without guile. There is a gentleness and even a long-suffering approach to living. They love life, people, and experience. What's the difference between these two contrasting modes of living?

The Art of Living with Love

Generally speaking, people who learn to take life's greatest lessons and pass them on to others are inspiring and motivating to nearly everyone. They understand the Law of Gratitude and develop the Art of Living with Love. They love life, challenges, growth, and others. They love the whole package! All of it! Life is happy and sometimes sad, but they love it. Life flows well at times, yet at others, the stony road of adversity raises its bruising head, and they continue to love it. There are also people who bring negativity and despondence, as well as those who help us to see its great blessings, and they love both kinds! Great people, the kind I want to be like, are those who live life with love. They live life loving it ... all of it!

Energizer One

WHO AM I? I am William Edward Otto Thorwald Christensen. I am W.C. Christensen, Junuis Cardon, Vaughn L. Christensen, and Irene Cardon. I am Deidre, Diane, and very much Deena. I am Dale, Adelaide, and Phylis. I am Mrs. Cheers, Frank Palmer, Coach Birdsong, and Carl Ferre. I am Doug, Perry, Willard, and Dennis. I am Earl, Alan, and Chuck. I am Tom and Paula. I am Dave Trexler. I am Doug, Jan, and Cindy. I am LeRoy, Mr. Salcido, Lindstrom, Jordan, Robert, Ray, Bruce, Brent, Duane, Ron, Dave, Alvin, and Don Powell. Rex and Charlene, David and Norma, as well as Terry, Ron, Bart, Alan, Max, and Andy. I am Brian, Reed, Lonny, Hobie, Billy, Amy, Sandy, and Adam. I am Gordon Romney, Joe J. Christensen, Ernest Skinner, Joseph Allen, Steve Bennion, Phil Wightman, and James Keller. I am Charles Hinds, Ririe Godfrey, Ellis Miller, Steve Terry, Andy Skinner, and Mark Bernsten. I am Greg Williams, Stan Stanley, Ferrell Young, Bob Hardy, Garth Olsen, Byron Webster, David Pack, Scott Mortensen, Greg Moeller, and Kevin Call. I am Scott Ferguson, Brent Strong, Gary Marshall, Wade Anderson, Gary Gardner, Thaine Robinson, Kris Fillmore, Fenton Broadhead, and Alan Hackworth. I am Mac Oswald, Jerry Burns, and Kelly Shepherd. I am Lowell Tingey and Tiny Grant. I am Wilborn Brown, Steve Phelps, Terry Seamons, Les Pospicil, Blair Packard, Wallace Slade, and Craig Cardon. I am Bryan Toone, Russ Thornock, Clate Mask, Wayne Guthrie, Steve Peterson, Gary Porter, David Cluff, and Ward Rasmussen. I am Malcom Pace, Larry Ferrin, and Larry Braithwaite. I am John Curtiss, Richard Smith, David Dorff, and Johnny West. I am Dale Miller, Steven Oveson, John Harris, Francisco Viñas, Curtis Bennett, Wayne Gardner, John Hadfield, Jose Garcia, David Hoopes, Ollie Smith, Kim Clark, Larry Thurgood, and David Bednar. I am Randy Garn, Ethan Willis, Aaron Peterson Jason Coulam, Blair Dance, and Travis Greene. I am Brad Parkinson, Craig Simpson, Fred Phillips, Todd Smith, Rick Neff, and Sheri Harrison. I am Simba, Alladin, and Quasimodo. I am very much Irvin,

Carole, Marv, Jan, Ken, Judy, Linda, Steve, Candace, Marvin, Alice, Craig, Lynette, Dru, Maureen, Mark, Leslie, John, Karlena, Dale, Julie, Kim, Pattie, Neil, Verlie, Shane, Vickie, and the list goes on and on—thousands of people. I am mostly Chantel, Creshel, Kit, Kieran, Karigan, Kimball, Aaron, Michelle, Taylor, Kylee, Jacob, Landon, Heber, Chalonn, McKay, London, Chelise, Chenae, Mat, Candra, and Devin.

WHO AM I? I am me ... David Alan Christensen!

I could add five hundred and sixty-three special colleages who touched my life as we labored together in South America, thousands of students and seminar participants, and many wonderful people who have shared an hour or two as a seat mate on an airplane, or engaged in telephonic dialing on some subject that's been mutually edifying. Tennyson once said, "I am a part of all that I have met." I have spent over five decades being around other people. Others really make up a significant part of my life. Everyone I have met and associated with have given something to my life. Even others who have joined me in circumstances which have been somewhat negative have instructed me, and I must forever understand that truly I am a part even of them. Both positive and negative, all who have touched my life have become a part of who I am today.

A handful of people will emerge as the great teachers in our lives. Those who have made great impact on "who we are" will usually be a just a few. Scores of others combine to make tiny strands of steel into strong and important cables of "who we have become." A few who have brushed our lives will have done so in the ardent furnaces of adverse conflict. Carefully examined however, even those situations will render tutorial verdicts in the building of one's life.

I am thankful for the great people in my life. As I look back at each one of the names mentioned earlier in this chapter, each contributed something to my life story. Some merit a chapter, others a paragraph or two, and others just a sentence; but all of them are a part of me.

Mrs. Cheers
I don't even know her first name and I haven't seen her for nearly forty years. She was a heavy woman with graying hair pulled back to a bun on the back of her head. She wore glasses, and more importantly, a wonderful caring smile. She was my second grade teacher. I can't remember specifically her contribution to the math score on my college entrance

exam or my ability to correctly spell the capital of each state. I do know that of all my teachers, she was my favorite. After all these years, I think the honor I give to her as one of the most important people in my life, has much to do with the way she put her large arm around my shoulder and kind of hugged me as she encouraged me to try again when I failed. She was nurturing and encouraging at a time when some others unintentionally conveyed a "you are behind the others" attitude toward me. I needed Mrs. Cheers! She was there to coax this little boy on to an understanding that he could do it! She seized each moment as a teaching opportunity in a way which others somehow missed. It is interesting to me that over the past two decades that my own life's path has been charted through a couple of professional changes, but I always come back to being a teacher. Even though I did not plan to become a teacher, my life's greatest moments have been centered in trying to be like Mrs. Cheers.

John Birdsong

What a coach! This man first beat me down to a level of humility so I would be teachable. Then he helped lift me to levels of performance I never dreamed of at that time of my life. I suppose I learned that "LOVE" of young men was really at the center of his coaching philosophy. He knew that his win-loss record (giving the school board a winning program) paled in significance when compared to building boys and making good men. He knew that in time the ecstasy of winning our Friday night game or qualifying for the State Tournament would soon fade into near forgotten memories. He knew that a victory over SELF would be forever! His short stocky stance, red face, and bald head will be forever in my mind. However, to teach me to admit to myself that I was falling short of my potential and then show me a way to crack through my self-imposed mental barriers, is seen almost everyday in the way I live my life. John Birdsong had an impact on my life!

Elena

This woman is an angel! "I'd rather see a sermon than hear one any day," my mother used to say. Elena is a sweet sermon of everything I want to become. I have observed her faith, compassion, and incredible sense of charity at moments when the masses turned another way. During her life's greatest challenges, such as a the tragic death and loss of her husband, a wayward child's actions against her, and a financial loss which altered her well-deserved security, she exhibited a spark of divinity. Always a smile and never a harsh word, even for those who she had every reason to seek restitution against or even destroy. I have met many others like her, who live their lives from a different perspective, while the masses embrace litigation and revenge as a way of life. Elena to me is a symbol of many others who have taught me about a higher way to live. I want to be like her!

The miracle of having "others" in our lives is tremendous. When we take time to think about what others have taught us and what strands of fiber they have contributed to who we are today, we are expanded. Our capacity to perform is increased, and our ability to be an important strand in someone else's life is heightened.

Exercise:

Perhaps the following list of questions will spawn some important names in your own census of great people in your life. Take fifteen minutes and write down the names of people who have made a difference in your life.

1. When you think of special people who have had an impact on your life, who comes immediately to your mind?

2. Sometimes we can learn a great deal from the mistakes of others. Can you think of someone who has taught you by their negative experiences, things you will want to avoid?

3. What friend, teacher, or speaker has made a change in the way you see life?

4. Have you ever experienced a "relationship fatality" where a friendship turned into an uncomfortable sense of hate, intolerance, or revenge? What happened that you can learn from? Can you now see a lesson that ought to be learned from the person involved?

5. Who are your greatest examples? Who are your heroes of important things? Who would you like to be more like?

Energizer Two

Life is experiential. Life is tutorial. The process of living produces many opportunities for discovery. If you examine your life, you will find that there are moments when your awareness was sharpened and your knowledge about life and it's purpose or meaning was heightened. Depending on your age you have been living somewhere between 7,000 and 25,000 days. During that time what have you learned about living—not making a living but about learning how to live? Can you identify five or ten important experiences in your life which have shaped who you are?

In the previous section of this chapter, the focus was on individual people who have made a difference. In this section, the focus is on experiences and processes of discovery. While people are almost always present, it is the experience that surfaces as the real teacher. Perhaps it was a negative experience with adversarial elements which served as a prologue to self-discovery.

Maybe it was an experience associated with divorce, financial stress, or social rejection. Maybe it was in making a team, excelling in music, finding a hidden talent with a paint brush, or discovering through experience that others find you easy to talk to and enjoy talking to you about their problems. Possibly an experience while traveling, climbing a mountain, or getting lost created a special learning experience for you. Conceivably, your grade school playground, or pushing yourself in a spelling bee, or seeing a friend hurt in some way have given you lifelong insights which will make a difference in your life. What are they?

I call these "switch points." Railroads have points in the tracks, which when switched, completely change the destination. These "switch points" are points in your life where you can see, in retrospect, that you changed course or discovered something which completely altered your direction. What are the "switch points" in your life? Can you identify a few and write them down?

Saying "NO" to a Seventh Grade Party

Do you remember what it was like to be in the seventh grade? Do you remember how important it was to be accepted? I do. I can see now that one the important "switch points" in my life came one Friday when one of my best school chums (a friend from kindergarten through sixth grade) invited me to a party. We had gone to a lot of birthday parties together, where we took presents, played Pin-the-Tail-on-the-Donkey, and ate cake and ice cream. My friend had an older brother who was one of the most popular ninth graders in the Jr. High School and hence, he (my friend) was being

---

launched into the "popular" crowd himself. His friendship meant a lot to me and my acceptance to the "in crowd" peer group at school.

My friend approached me at our locker and told me about a party to be held at a girl's house. "Her parents are out of town, and we will have a blast," he said. He told me that a mixed group of twenty to thirty would be attending, and we would really have some fun! (I could tell that he was not talking about playing Pin-the-Tail-on-the-Donkey) He told me that only the popular kids would be there, and a certain girl wanted to know if I was coming. When he told me who that "certain girl" was, my heart about jumped out of my chest. I was beginning to notice the physical changes going on in the girls we used to chase in the third grade. I confess I had noticed she was what I would have termed then as a real "fox." Everything seemed perfect! A private party, the popular set, and a budding young "fox" who expressed interest in my attendance. Naturally, I said, "I'll be there!" Somehow as the day proceeded and the between class chatter in the halls centered around the upcoming evening party, things seemed less and less perfect. Something didn't feel right. How would I tell my parents, who always insisted on knowing who I was with and where I would go? "I could tell them I was going to the movies or to a school game," I thought. Somehow I sensed that if I was going to need to lie to them about it, then maybe something wasn't really right about going. All day I struggled internally. I kept thinking of the cute girl who was going to be there. I started thinking about what twenty kids would do for three or four hours at a home where there were no adults. I started wondering if I should go. I struggled and struggled.

When it came time to go, I called my friend and told him I wouldn't be going. After a minute or two of coaxing and encouraging, he gave up and said "Okay, but you'll miss a lot of fun!" I did miss out. On Monday every-one was talking about all the "fun" they had. They somehow procured liqueur and they laughed about how each of them drank a little and that one of the girls drank a little too much and got tipped and silly. My friend chided me about the "foxy" girl having a great time with another guy. I saw them walking together in the hall later that day. While something made me feel good that I wasn't at the party, another side of me wished I had gone.

During the next few weeks, I noticed I wasn't quite a part of the "in crowd" group. There were other parties, and I wasn't invited to them. My friend and I began to drift apart, and our only real common bond was in the memories of the past. At times I felt like a "nerd" when they didn't include me in their social rendezvous. At other times, I enjoyed my own set of new friends who were a little more conservative and traditional in their social activities.

Looking back, I can see how that "switch point" brought me along a very different track through the high school years and to this point in my life. My friend and many in the popular group have struggled with alcoholism, drugs, broken marriages, and even prison (for a couple of my old grade school buddies). Hindsight tells me that day in my life was a very important "switch point." Things could be very different had I gone to the party and built my life around that peer group.

Porter Park

During my second year of college, I was particularly perplexed about a crossroads I was facing. I will spare the details of my dilemma, but suffice it to say that this particular crossroads was one of the most important forks in my road of life. I drove my car to the edge of a moderately large park in the small college town where I was living. It was early winter and the season's first major snowfall had started earlier in the day. The snow was nearly twelve inches deep and was still falling in large fluffy flakes. I wasn't particularly fond of the town or of the wintry, windy, blizzard-like conditions which that area of the country is known for. But this night was different. There was no wind and the temperature was not frigid—just falling snow and peace on earth. A large streetlight lit my way toward the interior of the park. I just walked, stopping occasionally to look up into the sky and watched the fleecy white flakes blanket everything in beautiful white. As far as I know, I was the only one in the park. The shroud of trees in the middle of the park prevented me from hearing the sound of cars on the streets surrounding this little piece of heaven on earth. I paused and sat on a bench. Everything was so beautiful, so still, so peaceful. The concerns of school, the dilemma about the girls I was currently dating, the condition of my bank account, and my pending draft to serve in the Vietnam War were all put on "hold." It was in this peaceful paradise that I was able to sort through and find the power to make my choice at the fork in the road and to have the courage to do it. Since then I have often thought of Robert Frosts classic poem "The Road Not Taken":

> Two roads diverged in a yellow wood,
> And sorry I could not travel both
> And be one traveler, long I stood

And looked down one as far as I could
To where it bent in the undergrowth;

Then took the other, as just as fair,
And having perhaps the better claim,
Because it was grassy and wanted wear;
Though as for that the passing there
Had worn them really about the same,

And both that morning equally lay In
leaves no step had trodden black.

Oh, I kept the first for another day!
Yet knowing how way leads on to say,
I doubted if I should ever come back.

I shall be telling this with a sigh
Somewhere ages and ages hence:
Two roads diverged in a wood, and I
I took the one less traveled by,
And that has made all the difference.

Though I spare the details of the fork in my road, I know that the decision of which road to follow has made all the difference in my life. My own choice came in "a wood" in the quiet peace of a white, pristine wonderland park in Southeastern Idaho. "And that has made all the difference."

What have been your crossroads? Which can you identify as life-changing and -shaping experiences? Identify and write them down.

Empire Crumbled

Years ago, a dear friend and I decided to become partners in building a business. Thousands of young entrepreneurs make the same choice and hold the same dream every day in this land of freedom. As with most "upstart" business ventures, the beginning was tough. But within a reasonable period of time the business began to prosper. Our choices brought success to ourselves and those we served. The business grew larger and served more people. We followed financial counsel to diversify our profits and channel our growth into multiple business interests which would give us more stability. However, the choice to spread our financial base over several interests, coupled with debtors who failed in their payments to us, a falling economy, and other unforeseen challenges resulted in our little empire collapsing! In the months that followed there were public humiliations, angry lenders, and a multiplicity of broken dreams.

This experience, though I regret that it affected others, was one of the most instructive prologues in my own personal discovery of life. I observed in those months a complete display of mankind's greatest and weakest attributes. Further, I was required to reach into the deepest chamber of my own heart and determine who I had been, who I was, and how I would react to the situation. It was in the hellish furnace of adversity that I came to know that while my choices and perspectives may have been shortsighted, ill advised, and regretful—in the sense that they adversely affected other lives— my character was clean. I knew, though others might think otherwise, that my motives were proper, my actions true, and my relationship with deity without blemish.

Have you had experiences in the crucible of adversity, misfortune, or pain where you have been taught? Think about them. Write them down. Be thankful for their place in your life. While no one seeks or desires setbacks and mountains of defeat, it is often in these moments and experiences that we find ourselves.

Jan

It was in the early winter of 1953 when I looked out the big window of our farm house toward the road. I was awaiting the arrival of my brothers and sisters from school. Today was special! The season's first snow was falling and covering the ground with several inches in our northwestern New Mexico town of Farmington. The town radio stations sponsored an annual "snow-guessing contest." All who wanted would guess the day and time of the season's first snowfall. The winners were awarded prizes from the merchants in town, ranging from free dinners at local restaurants, to tires, clock radios, clothing, candy, groceries, and auto maintenance needs. Our family never missed entering the annual challenge but had never even come close to winning. This day was different! Today we were sure to win. My older brother Marv had chosen this day for the snow to fall, cover the ground, and meet the other specifications of the contest rules. We knew he would win—which meant all of us would win!

Finally, five other siblings arrived home. While Mom stayed by the radio to listen for the announcement of the winner, we went out to play in the snow. Finally, Mom called us to the covered porch and disclosed the bad news. Someone else had won! After forty-eight seconds of dismay, we gleefully returned to making angels in the snow, building a snow man, and playing in the fluffy white stuff.

Mother called us in from the winter playground of our front lawn to eat supper. During the meal my older brother, age ten, complained of aching muscles and fatigue. After dinner, my great little mother, who was expecting her seventh child, put Marv to bed for needed rest. The next morning he was too sick to go to school. Later in the day, one of my older sisters telephoned from school complaining of aching muscles and tiredness, and asked if someone could bring her home. Two days later, the situation repeated itself with another older sister. Now three of the six children in my family were sick at home. I thought it was great! As a three year old, I was just happy I didn't have to be home alone.

A visit from the doctor rendered an announcement to my parents that would temporarily wreck their lives and change their perspectives forever. Three of their six children were stricken with the dreaded disease polio. While I was too young to appreciate what was going on, I can imagine what the news would do to any parent. Imagine the fear they felt wondering about the outcomes of this crippling disease upon those they loved most. There also was a financial concern in those struggling years about the cost of medical care.

Little did my parents know that the stage was just being set. The following ten days would unveil the preface to a story that they never imagined possible in this little family. A quarantine was place on our home which allowed only the doctor to come and go. Within a few days Jan was rushed by airplane to specialized care in Albuquerque and Carole soon joined her.

Being only three years old at the time, I remember very little. But I did feel the vacancies at our family dinner table, which was normally a place of cheer, discussion of the days activities, and comments about Mother's wonderful cooking. The long, lonely days passed with Mother gone to Albuquerque to be with her two eldest children in the polio ward of Carrie Tingley Hospital. Soon the Christmas season arrived. Marvin had completely recuperated, but Jan and Carole remained in Albuquerque with Mother at their bedside. Jan's condition had worsened to the degree that she was placed in an iron lung.

One December evening at our nearly vacant dinner table with just five of the eight eating bread and milk, Dad announced we would all be going to the hospital to be with Mom, Carole, and Jan. He said we would be leaving the day before Christmas and travel the two hundred miles after he finished the afternoon chores on our small dairy farm. At the announcement I was so happy. It seemed like an eternity since our family had been separated by this disease.

On Christmas Eve afternoon, I remember loading the old slope-back Chevrolet with a few homemade gifts and a whole bunch of cheer. As we drove the two hundred miles it was decided that, in addition to the few gifts we had assembled for them, I would be taught a silly little verse as a special present to my two older sisters. My older siblings decided I must present it to them by memory. Now that seems simple enough, but for a three-year-old, the verse made absolutely no sense and seemed to never end.

"Hey kid are you the kid that went around the corner kid, no kid I'm not the kid that went around the corner kid, then who is the kid that went around the corner kid ... I dunno kid? Are you the kid that went around the corner kid, no kid I'm not the kid that went around the corner kid, then who is the kid ... ?" It can go on forever! See what I mean? This is a no-brainer! As I tried to learn the pattern I struggled through the lines and stumbled on nearly every word. "Hey kid on the corner, did you see that other boy ... ?" My brothers and sisters would laugh and mimic and coax me to try again, and again, and again. Somehow two hundred miles, which normally seemed the distance to the moon, went very quickly that evening. My coaches and teachers were finally successful in their bid to prepare me, their little moon-faced brother, to present my gift to my big sisters on Christmas morning.

We stayed that evening in a motel and enjoyed a warm Christmas Eve. The holidays anticipation which was normally characterized by whispers and questions about Santa Claus and all the things we were going to receive from the jolly old fellow, was replaced by discussion and excitement of seeing and being with our older sisters the following morning. As usual, Christmas Eve night passed very slowly, but finally Christmas morning came. Dad scraped the frost from the car window, and we noisily loaded into the car for our short trip to the hospital. On the way, my older siblings coached me and helped polish the verse I had learned. I was excited, and I was ready!

We entered the big sterile building and walked down the corridors. Our steps seemed to echo as we moved down the hall into the room where the polio patients were. I remember entering the room and hearing the eerie noises of the iron lung machines, as they manipulated the breathing of the patients. I remember the rocking beds which were to assist the less severe patients with the breathing process. In fact, I remember wishing I had a bed like that and how fun it must be to live in such a playground of interesting equipment. The nurse pointed to an iron lung which to me, had the appearance of a small submarine with an oxygen tent draped over one end. "Here's Jan, and I will go get Carole," she announced. We all gathered together around Carole's bed and the iron lung containing Jan. Finally we were all together, reunited after a nearly a whole month! I remember close and happy feelings. I remember nothing about Santa Claus or expensive Christmas toys, because there were none. But I do recall the happy, joyful feelings that come when really important things happen. Our family was together! We were smiling and enjoying just being together. Our inexpensive, homemade gifts were unwrapped along with many others given by good and charitable people from the community. Then Marvin blurted out, almost as an afterthought, that there was one more gift yet to be given. Someone said "Yes, we've saved the best for last." The room grew quiet and a small stool was placed for me to stand at the side of the iron lung and near the end of Carole's bed. I took my place, looking at both sisters, but mostly at Jan inside that iron lung. I took a big deep breath, and with a grin on my face I began, ... "Hey kid are you the kid that went around the corner kid? No kid, I'm not the kid that went around the corner kid ..." I went on and on and on. As I repeated it without a flaw, looked into the eyes of these two great sisters and saw smiles. Tears welled-up in their eyes, and I somehow knew that they were not sad tears, rather happy ones. I knew they had accepted my gift, and even at that tender age of three, I felt I was making a difference in their lives. I was making a difference for those who had loved me, and I felt great love for them. That was a special day. I have found those same feelings each time I extend myself to another human being and "make a difference" in their day. In fact, the great moments in my life have come when I get outside myself and give something which costs no money. Giving a little bit of "me" somehow gives that sense of inner joy that cannot be found anywhere else.

The memory of this experience energizes me to action every time I recall it. You have such experiences. Find them and write them down. Like boosters on a rocket engine, your life will accelerate in positive directions as you build on great moments in your living experiences. Your life will be sweeter and more fulfilled.

Energizer Three

Perhaps one of the most energizing, healing, and beneficial experiences of gaining personal power comes from a process known as forgiveness. Historically, every culture woven with the ethics of Buddhism, Judaism, Islam, Shinto, Christianity, or other religious thought, has taught the value of forgiving and letting go of negative issues which enter our lives. There is something inherent in harboring ill feelings towards other people or events that has a retarding, debilitating, binding and damning effect upon our growth and development. Conversely, there is power that comes to anyone who will release harbored feelings, and redirect the energy of hate and ill will toward productive living. Life, with its complexities, is hard enough without being subservient to issues which sap important energy and thought away from a happy life.

Once a man said to me "David, I completely and totally forgive . Life is too short and too sweet to spend it in hate and ill will." That is truth! Life is too short and too sweet to allow ill feelings toward others, remorse over past deeds, or to detour our life in alternate back roads. Spending time and energy against another for something they did or didn't do, being angry at God or fate for our circumstances, or spending life disliking ourselves for actions in a weak moment, is like carrying around a hundred pound bag of cobble rocks twenty-four hours a day. That's dumb! Besides, it's a burden! If you are carrying a bag of rocks—ill will toward another person, resentment for some stroke of bad luck, or unresolved remorse for some deed in your own life— it's time to unload! While it may take time beyond the momentary decision to forgive, get started on the road toward forgiveness and freedom.

These things are often far too personal to share with everyone. This is one area where I choose not to give personal examples to help you identify your bag of rocks and how to unload them. I will admit that in my first experience with this exercise, I said to myself "No, not me! I don't have any bad feelings toward anyone ... I hold no grudges!" Closer inspection revealed a few rocks I'd been carrying around for twenty years. I had become so accustomed to their weight, that I didn't even recognize they were there. 'When I came face to face with them and unloaded, the reduced weight gave me unbelievable, new-found strength. I was energized!

The process of scanning your life for rocks of hate or ill will is challenging, but worth it. The rocks are often found in our closest relationships. Crazy little things, like feeling that Mom or Dad loved or cared for your sibling more than they did you. Or perhaps someone was not sensitive to your feelings, and publicly embarrassed you or privately criticized your actions.

Research bears out that the number-one person blamed for life's greatest tests or challenges is Deity. God seems to get credit for all the negative things that happen to us. Are you feeling even a little resentful for some stroke of bad luck and continue to wonder why God didn't deliver you in the way you felt was right? Is there someone who seems always to have the good luck—promotions, inheritance, a more direct superhighway to success, and the good things; while you have to drive the backroads, dead-end streets, detours, and highways always under construction? Do you find anyone or any situation that makes you feel uncomfortable when you see them or come face-to-face? Do you still feel anger toward anyone who has treated you wrong? Are you jealous of someone because they seem to have all the luck, more friends, more money, more toys, more attention, more popularity, and an undeserved better life than you? Do you have angry feelings toward well-meaning parents who made unintentional mistakes in their efforts to be the best they could be? Have you blamed God, destiny, or your astrological sign for any of life's misfortunes? Has anyone ever violated you, taken advantage of you, or been inconsiderate of your feelings? Do you continue to hold a grudge? Have you ever violated another person, passed gossip, been unkind, spoken cruel words, or hurt others in any way? If so, are you willing to take the first step toward seeking forgiveness and mending the relationship? Scan your heart and mind for those rocks and unload even the pebbles! If you are normal, this is not a one-stop trash dump at the landfill. It is an exercise which takes time and an attitude of keeping your bag free of any new stones as well.

Summary

These three energizers, when given proper attention, will add a dimension that you never thought possible to your capacity to perform. They come from a deep sense of thankfulness and an attitude of gratitude for people, life's experiences, and for your own innate abilities to reach more lofty ideals. When we "think thanks," we acknowledge life as a well-defined school. Everything that is taught in the school is helpful to our growth, and nothing is negative! We, therefore, are students participating in positive discovery. "Think Thanks!" and take the time to write your feelings down so that you can enjoy the thought processes over and over again. These activities added upon will bring to your life energy and perspective not heretofore enjoyed. They are truly energizers!

ASSIGNMENT

Identify:

1. Others in your life who have made a difference. Write a brief paragraph or two about what specific thing they taught or inspired in you. There will likely be many, so for now, identify five or ten, and tell why they are so important to you. You can add others to your list in the weeks, months, and years ahead.

2. Experiences or "switch points" in your life, where the experience itself taught you lessons about living. Again, there may be many. For now, select only three or four major experiences in your life which have influenced your outcomes positively.

3. Situations, circumstances, actions, or people toward whom you are expending negative energy. Identify them and then process, in your own mind, how you can best "let go" and forget about the issue forever. Make a conscious effort to bury the past mistake, deed, or attitude which causes you to be negatively influenced. Bury it! Many people carry few or none of these burdens. That's good! Others can identify several people or events that fuel the furnace of the heart and arouse negative feelings. It is time to BURY THEM!

Chapter Fourteen

SING YOUR OWN SONG

I have lived in a part of the country where seasonally there is a lot of snow. There have been years when the snowfall has been incredibly significant and our backyard accumulates much of the drifting flakes. I don't always enjoy the cold and the necessity of dedicating part of my life to shoveling the white stuff from my driveway. Not long ago I was removing several feet of snow from our large deck. The task took several hours. While I labored, I thought about the accumulation of the millions of snowflakes on my deck, a relatively micro spot on earth. I remembered something my university professor had emphasized decades earlier when he said "there are no two snowflakes which are identical." If I had a million or two snowflakes on my deck, think of the number of snowflakes covering the vast Arctic, Antarctic, and mountain glaciers. The thought is staggering!

My thoughts moved from snow to sand and stars to human fingerprints and DNA. Isn't it incredible to know that everything has its own identity? Since the first cell split, the second did not look quite like the first. A rattlesnake is not only different than a cobra, but it's different than any other rattlesnake. Millions of cobras have common characteristics with billions of earthworms, yet they are all functionally and extraordinarily different. There are no two identical pine trees or palms. Rats are different than hamsters, and hamsters are different than gerbils, although they look somewhat alike. Yet within their species, phylums, and genders, every single one is just a wee bit different. Years ago I heard a speaker quote an unknown poet. Though I have already used it in this book, I think it is appropriate to draw attention to it again.

> Every blade of grass,
> And every flake of snow
> Are just a wee bit different.
> There's no two alike, you know.
>
> From something small like grains of sand
> To each gigantic star,
> Each one was made with this in mind
> To be just what they are.

How foolish then to imitate,
How useless to pretend,
When each one of us comes from a mind
Whose ideas never end.

There'll only be just one of me
To show what I can do
And likewise you should feel very proud
There's only one of you.

Author Unknown

Each of us comes to earth with a special capacity to write and sing our own song. Too often, our environment may send the message that we need to be more like everyone else, to lose our identity and the power to contribute our song. We may confuse who we are and what our individual part is, in the choral group of the family of man. Society may even perpetuate the erroneous notion that our song has more to do with what we own and possess, than it does with the solo we sing or the harmony we bring to the chorus.

The purpose of this book has been twofold. It is dedicated to people in transition. It is to assist in the process of changing, developing personally, aiding in a transformation. It is to assist the reader in the realignment process each of us face at transitional times in our lives. It has been an invitation to look into your character, not your personality—to find the uniqueness of who you are and what you can contribute.

Hopefully, understanding that public victories are preceded by private or inner victories, will put you in the winner's column more often. You have been given principles to facilitate your quest to have more inner victories. You have been invited to look inside yourself and discover who you are. Finding your uniqueness in beliefs, values, goals, and energy to succeed are fundamental to your transition and realignment process. Finding your uniqueness and being willing to confidently and courageously "sing your own song" to the world around you is the objective of this whole exercise.

This is not a "read a book" exercise. This is the beginning of your "interior design" course where you look inward and design the kind of life you will be extraordinarily happy with, because it makes a difference in the lives of others. If you are a student, I know that you will do better in school if you have this sense of identity and inner peace. Your classes will become more relevant and your learning more focused in the enhancement of your song. Your transition to college and then from college to the professional, career world will be more meaningful. If you are in any of a myriad of mid-life transitional concerns, such as career change, divorce, health battles, or relocation—I believe with all my heart, the concepts we have reviewed in this book will bless your life. Your realignments and new beginnings will assist you to be more alive and awake. You will be able to sing your song in the next chapters of your life with more clarity and harmony. Your life will be better!

I am interested in who you are and what you have found in this book which will help you in your life. I invite you to write a brief letter to me, David A. Christensen, at www.davidachristensen.com. Share with me what you have enjoyed most about this exercise. If you want to request additional information, reading lists or bibliographies, be sure to state your request clearly. I hope that in the course of time, you will be able to account some of your personal inner and public victories to what you gleaned from this work.

Now, Sing Your Song! Sing it in the best way you know how. Be glad you are who you are, and Sing Your Song! In the words of Douglas Malloch:

> If you can't be a pine on the top of the hill
> Be a scrub in the valley—but be
> The best little scrub by the side of the hill;
> Be a bush if you can't be a tree.
>
> If you can't be a bush be a bit of the grass,
> And some highway some happier make;
> If you can't be a muskie then just be a bass
> But be the liveliest bass in the lake!
>
> We can't all be captains, we've got to be crew,
> There's something for all of us here.
> There's a big work to do and there's lesser to do,
> And the task we must do is near.
>
> If you can't be a highway then just be a trail,
> If you can't be the sun be a star;
> It isn't by size that you win or you fail
> Be the best at whatever you are!

Be the Best of Whatever You Are (copyright © 1925 by the McClure Newspaper Syndicate).

Sing your song! Sing it clear! Be the best you can be and know that within you, your experiences, your challenges, your unique success, your contribution to your piece of the world will be significant! You'll make a difference! As the writer Ralph Waldo Emerson wrote, "Insist on yourself, never imitate.

ASSIGNMENT

1. Write down your "song." This is the mission statement for your life. Whether it's a paragraph, one page or many is not important. The important thing is to identify the elements which your life stands for. What will you be remembered for?

2. Sometimes people find it helpful to create a visual image of their "song" (mission). Developing a crest, a collage, or some symbol which visually identifies who they are and what they will represent in life.

You now have a blueprint to build and live your life by. This Creed Document will be the basis for your transition and decisions for life. If you will review it often and inspect yourself periodically in light of its direction, life's transitions and changes will be executed with less trauma. You will find that your life takes on much more focus and your energy will be channeled into positive movement. The process of creating this document has assisted you in aligning who you are with what you believe and value. Going through each step has helped you to transform your thinking. You have experienced the beginning of new development and growth. Your transition from wherever you were, to where you want to be, is beginning to take place. It will be accelerated as you use this important tool in designing and creating your life according to the specifications your inner self has identified as YOU.

Transition is wonderful! It is also a constant part of living. Encounter each transition with a feel for your "song" and a vision of the life you desire. You will find your actions "sing" who and what you are to others.

Have a happy life, filled with joy and inner peace. Enjoy your INNER VICTORIES!